CASE STUDIES IN ENTREPRENEURSHIP

The authors dedicate this book to Marlene's husband, Bill, and Rochelle's husband, Kirk. These two men have always enthusiastically supported our academic endeavors.

CASE STUDIES IN ENTREPRENEURSHIP

MARLENE M. REED

D.B.A, Entrepreneur in Residence, Department of Entrepreneurship and Corporate Innovation, Hankamer School of Business, Baylor University, USA

ROCHELLE R. BRUNSON

PhD, Clinical Associate Professor for Apparel Merchandising, Department of Human Sciences and Design, Robbins College of Health and Human Sciences, Baylor University, USA

Edward Elgar
PUBLISHING

Cheltenham, UK • Northampton, MA, USA

Cover image: Dr. Danielle Young

Published by
Edward Elgar Publishing Limited
The Lypiatts
15 Lansdown Road
Cheltenham
Glos GL50 2JA
UK

Edward Elgar Publishing, Inc.
William Pratt House
9 Dewey Court
Northampton
Massachusetts 01060
USA

A catalogue record for this book
is available from the British Library

Library of Congress Control Number: 2021938666

This book is available electronically in the **Elgar**online
Business subject collection
http://dx.doi.org/10.4337/9781839101427

Printed on elemental chlorine free (ECF)
recycled paper containing 30% Post-Consumer Waste

ISBN 978 1 83910 141 0 (cased)
ISBN 978 1 83910 143 4 (paperback)
ISBN 978 1 83910 142 7 (eBook)

Printed and bound in the USA

CONTENTS

Acknowledgments   vi

Introduction to *Case Studies in Entrepreneurship*   1

1   Beginning with an idea – Warby Parker: revolutionizing the way
eyeglasses are sold and social entrepreneurship is carried out   2

2   Entrepreneurial mindset – WeWork: can a shared space provider
survive a recession?   11

3   Recognizing a good opportunity – White Trash Services: targeting
a new market?   18

4   Planning for the long run – Rakuten: how long can rapid growth be sustained? 28

5   Securing funding – Kickstarter: creating a platform for crowdfunding dreams   38

6   Securing funding (continued) – Nightlight Donuts: the trials of
a collegiate entrepreneur   49

7   Developing a new business model – Etsy: will the desire for economic
success overwhelm creativity?   57

8   Assessing the role of the entrepreneur – Revival Restaurant: revitalizing
a dormant neighborhood   66

9   Maintaining a business during a recession – Kleinfeld Bridal: absolutely "yes"! 74

10 Attaining long-term success – Magnolia and The Silos: sustaining rapid
growth   84

11 Exploring new business – Lily Jade: developing an online apparel
business driven by social media   92

12 Starting a social enterprise – The TLC Rocket Stove: results-based
financing through carbon credits   101

13 The role of a first mover – *The Fleet Sheet:* seeking sustainability for
a first mover   113

14 Preparing an exit strategy – BCH TeleCommunications: an American
ex-patriot deciding when and how to leave the Czech Republic   122

Index   131

ACKNOWLEDGMENTS

The authors would like to thank the entrepreneurs whom they interviewed to obtain information for the cases written about their businesses. They also appreciate the additional time the entrepreneurs spent reviewing and correcting the cases, where needed, and supplying pictures of their businesses to enrich the case experience for the students.

Introduction to *Case Studies in Entrepreneurship*

After attending many conferences on entrepreneurship and talking to colleagues at other universities, it occurred to the authors that there was a need for a book that would contain current entrepreneurship cases of special interest to students. Most entrepreneurship and small business textbooks contain few, if any, cases that an instructor can dig into with students and illustrate important theories or topics from the course. That realization was the impetus for writing this casebook.

Most of the cases in this book have been class tested, and often the instructor's manual was revised after this experience. The Warby Parker, Etsy and Magnolia and the Silos cases were entrepreneurial endeavors the students already know something about; and they enjoyed expressing their views on challenges the entrepreneurs faced. The Lily Jade, Nightlight Donuts and Revival Restaurant cases were entirely new to students, but they were intrigued by the way in which each of these entrepreneurs recognized an opportunity for a new business.

We hope you will enjoy developing your students' critical thinking skills as you explore these new cases with them.

Online resources to supplement the book can be accessed at: https://www.e-elgar.com/textbooks/reed?stage=Stage.

1

Beginning with an idea – Warby Parker: revolutionizing the way eyeglasses are sold and social entrepreneurship is carried out

http://www.warby-parker.com/

Donating can create dependencies. Therefore, it is important to not donate but support poor people in order to create business structures.[1]

With this statement, the founders of Warby Parker disrupted the traditional social entrepreneurship model of "buy-one, give-one" by launching the company in 2010. By 2020, the co-CEOs, David Gilboa and Neil Blumenthal, had achieved a value of $1.7 billion for the company and expanded their initial exclusive operations of selling eyeglasses on the internet to include 90 physical stores in the United States and Canada. With such success for their business, the CEOs knew they would have to continue to innovate to stay one step ahead of the copy-cat eyeglass competitors.

BACKGROUND ON WARBY PARKER

In the summer of 2008, David Gilboa was backpacking around the world before he started to graduate school. Unfortunately, he lost his glasses on a plane and delayed buying a pair in his first semester in school because eyeglasses were so expensive. He found it hard to believe that he could buy a new phone for $200, but a pair of designer glasses cost $700.[2]

Gilboa and Blumenthal and the two other founders, Andrew Hunt and Jeffrey Raider, were all students at the Wharton School at the University of Pennsylvania, and they began kicking around an idea for an online operation that would sell inexpensive yet stylish eyeglasses. One of the founders sent around a three-page email about the business idea, and the other three responded to it.

Before long, each of the founders had taken the lead on some part of the operation. Gilboa built the website, set up the supply chain, hired the first employee, set up a phone system and a customer service system. Blumenthal worked on branding and drew up a mission and values statement. The founders utilized focus groups in the beginning to determine if the idea for the business would capture the attention of their potential customers. They were trying to understand the business model of Luxottica and the other large optical retailers. Each of the founders put in $30,000 for the startup of the business. The company was launched in 2010 while all four of the founders were still in school.[3] The venture also received $2,500 as seed money from The Venture Initiation Program at the Wharton School. The name Warby Parker was derived from two characters in a novel by Jack Kerouac—Warby Pepper and Zagg Parker.

The founders chose JAND Inc. as their corporate name. Because of their low price point and classy product, the company surpassed their first year's sales target within three weeks after launch. The business sold out of its top 15 sellers in just four weeks and had a waiting list of 20,000 names. All of this was accomplished without any paid advertising.[4] By May of 2011, the company had shipped more than 100,000 pairs of glasses and had 60 employees. By the end of 2012, the company had expanded to 100 employees.

BACKGROUND ON GILBOA AND BLUMENTHAL

David Gilboa

Gilboa was born in Sweden, and his parents were both doctors. When he was a teenager, David would often go with his father to the hospital to learn all that he could about medical specialties. At the time, he intended to study medicine and become a doctor. However, when he was a premed student at the University of California, Berkeley, he found out about HMOs and that led to a decision to seek another career. After leaving medical school, he worked for Bain Capital and later for the investment bank Allen & Co. He later returned to school at the University of Pennsylvania to get a master's degree in biomedical engineering and an MBA at the Wharton School. It was there that he met the other co-founders of Warby Parker. Blumenthal referred to him as "the smart one."[5]

Neil Blumenthal

Blumenthal was the son of a tax consultant and a nurse. He grew up in Greenwich Village and had always had an entrepreneurial streak. When he was only 8 years old, he convinced his parents to buy him a food dehydrator so that he could begin a dried fruits stand on Mercer Street. In high school, he was a club promoter at a local night club.

Blumenthal attended Tufts University and had a double major in international relations and history. At this point, he wanted to be the Secretary of State of the United States. After college, he had a fellowship in El Salvador and helped develop the market-based approach to philanthropy at VisionSpring. Blumenthal suggested, "I was trying to understand how we could get entrepreneurs to spend more time selling glasses, doing margin analysis, going over to China to try to source glasses at lower cost."[6] All of these experiences prepared him for his work at Warby Parker.

MISSION

The mission of Warby Parker is to offer designer eyeglasses at a revolutionary price, while leading the way for socially conscious businesses.

VALUE PROPOSITION

The company vows to offer low price but high quality that can be achieved by vertical integration and cutting out the middleman. They design the glasses in-house and sell them directly to the customer.

THE PRODUCT

One of the initial problems the CEOs ran into was the issue of customers not being able to try on their products since they were buying them on the internet. To get around this challenge, the company decided to send each customer five pairs of frames to try on and select a favorite design. The customer was required to return the glasses within five days. This convenient option did not have a charge attached to it so it allowed a customer to try on the frames at home just as they would in the store. Some of their eye wear sold for as little as $95. By the establishment of this process of selling inexpensive glasses online, Warby Parker became a disrupter in the eyeglass industry (see Figure 1.1 entitled "Eyeglasses" and Figure 1.2 entitled "Sunglasses.")

Source: This photo by unknown author is licensed under CC BY-SA; this license is free by the licensor.

Figure 1.1   Eyeglasses

Figure 1.2   Sunglasses

Copy-cats

The business model adopted by Warby Parker was very easy to replicate. The process had been followed by companies selling products from mattresses to men's shoes. There were a few companies that were complete copy-cats and did everything that Warby Parker did. These companies were EyeFly, Made Eyewear, and Jimmy Fairly. However, even though they had adopted the business model of Warby Parker, they had not received the attention and the sales of this company. Joel Cutler, a co-founder of the venture firm General Catalyst Partners and an investor in Warby Parker said, "Neil and Dave are inventing this idea of what a technology-based lifestyle brand is."[7]

Outsourcing

David Gilboa suggested that the best advice he could give about the development of a product was to never outsource critical components of your business. In supporting that advice, he said:

> None of us were qualified to build the website, so we solicited proposals and got a handful of bids from agencies. We chose the cheapest option, but a few months in, we realized that it was a mistake. Their execution wasn't what they promised, so we fired them.[8]

After that experience, they decided to develop all of their technology within the company to give the customer the best possible experience.

The company ordered its own materials from Italy, and one of the biggest inputs for the glasses was acetate. Originally, they had their glasses manufactured in China, but in 2017 they opened an optical lab in Rockland County, New York, in order to produce their own glasses and ==ensure the quality that== they desired. The lab contained 34,000 square feet and employed 130 people.

Not all CEOs believed that the smartest way to run a company was to avoid outsourcing. Debra Cohen, founder of Home Remedies of New York, a home improvement contract referral service, outsourced all of her operations. She had only one employee, and Cohen concentrated on sales, business development, and screening home improvement vendors. Even her web development and maintenance, graphic design, software development, and financial record keeping were outsourced. Cohen suggested, "Stick to what you are good at and outsource everything else."[9]

Employees *everything is tightly managed*

To preserve the free-wheeling spirit of the founders, when potential employees were interviewed, they were asked, "When was the last time you wore a costume?" After they were hired, the employees area asked to fill out a "15 Five" report every week explaining what they accomplished in the past week, their plans for the coming week, and a suggestion for an innovative idea. The model for hiring employees at Warby Parker was not Zappo's but Bain Capital. The employees for their call center were hired directly out of college and were expected to answer phone calls for a couple of years before rising within the organization.[10] Since eyeglasses were high-grossing products, the company was able to pay their call center employees well.

All of the new employees at Warby Parker were given a copy of Jack Kerouac's book entitled *The Dharma Bums* and a copy of the *Style Guide* which included suggestions about usage and grammar. The *Guide* also encouraged employees, when they communicated with customers, to write like Warby Parker was the person you'd want to be next to you at a dinner party.[11]

E-COMMERCE VS. BRICK-AND-MORTAR STORES

Warby Parker opened its first brick-and-mortar store in 2013 after launching their products online in 2011. The intention of the company was to further develop their brand with the retail stores. In 2015, they extended their brand further by partnering with Nordstrom to develop "pop up shops" around the country.

Sucharita Mulpurn, a retail analyst, suggested that since 90 percent of retail still takes place in brick-and-mortar stores, this decision by Warby Parker made a lot of sense. She further explained:

> There's an argument that when you're a private label and people don't necessarily know who you are, letting them touch and feel your products can be critical in reducing any friction.[12]

Neil Blumenthal sees the future of retailing as a convergence of brick-and-mortar and e-commerce. In order to serve their customers more efficiently, they came up with a procedure by which customers could book an appointment online to have an eye exam. Then when they entered the store, they would see a large digital screen that displayed the time of the appointment. The screen was fashioned after train station boards with updates every 15 minutes.[13]

THE EYEGLASS INDUSTRY

This industry produces eyeglasses, contact lens and sunglasses. One of the key drivers is the aging population because as people get older they tend to need corrective lenses. Another driver is funding by Medicare and Medicaid and private insurance. Whenever there is an increase in federal funding for Medicare and Medicaid, the demand for corrective lenses also increases. Federal funding for these two programs was expected to increase in 2019. The growth in the number of people covered by private health insurance was expected to slow in the next few years following 2019. *Need a weird in-between*

An increase in per capita disposable income allows people to spend more money on items that are not essential such as eyeglass frames. Growth in disposable income was expected to increase in 2019. Eyeglass and contact lens manufacturing contracted over the five years leading to 2019. Some of the reasons for this slowed performance was the strength of the dollar which boosted the importation of glasses from abroad. However, with the increase in disposable income, and private health insurance coverage, consumers have been visiting optometrists more frequently, resulting in greater demand for these products. To remain competitive, American producers have had to alter their business strategies to meet the increase in imports.

After suffering from years of decline, revenue growth in the United States increased 0.20 percent in 2018 and 2.0 percent in 2019. The outlook was for zero growth in revenue in 2020 and above 1.0 percent growth in 2021 and 2022.[14]

LUXOTTICA

This vertically integrated Italian company designed as well as manufactured eye wear. By 2019, the company had a 40 percent market share in the eyeglass industry. Luxottica operated in 150 countries and 8,000 retail locations. The company's primary retail operations were LensCrafters and Pearle Vision chain stores. In its sunglass division, the company operated through the Sunglass Hut and Oakley stores. The primary focus of operations of the company was in the mid- to premium-priced eye wear. The leading house brand was Ray-Ban, but they also offered glasses under the name Prada, Dolce & Gabbana, Polo Ralph Lauren and Chanel.

In the years leading up to 2019, the company had concentrated on reducing their costs, closing underperforming stores and refining their product portfolio to move into higher-end offerings. However, the mid- and premium-priced categories were vulnerable to consumer preferences and economic downturns.[15]

THE SOCIAL ENTREPRENEURSHIP MODEL

The founders of Warby Parker resisted following the traditional "buy-one, give-one" model made famous by Tom's Shoes. With this model, each time a customer bought a pair of shoes from Tom's, the company supplied a second pair of shoes for someone in need—normally in a Third World country. The problem with this model was that this cut out many entrepreneurs selling shoes in the country in which the shoes were furnished. Thus, a backlash was created in the country against a company that was hurting the development of small businesses.

Warby Parker altered this approach to social entrepreneurship by setting up a program whereby when a pair of glasses was purchased from their company, they would pay for the production of another pair of glasses for the non-profit organization VisionSpring. Then VisionSpring would sell the glasses to companies in developing countries so that entrepreneurship would be supported in that country. The social entrepreneurship portion of their mission was added when the founders discovered that approximately 10 percent of the world's population needed glasses but did not have them. VisionSpring also trained low-income entrepreneurs to sell the glasses in their villages.

Another part of their social entrepreneurship program was the Pupil Project. Such dignitaries as Gloria Steinem and Iman designed some of the glasses used in the program. The Pupil Project furnished screenings, eye exams, and attractive glasses to students who could not afford a pair on their own. David Gilboa said of the project, "There's nothing like watching these students, many of whom are getting their first pair of glasses, finally see the board clearly."[16]

The famous model Iman decided to participate in the program because she speculated, "So often we take the gift of sight for granted. We just assume that when we hone in on something, it will come through with crystal clarity. However, when we need to improve our vision, it often comes with a price that is virtually unaffordable to most."[17]

The project by 2018 had already delivered 46,000 pairs of glasses to 150 public elementary and middle schools in Baltimore.

Normally a social entrepreneur is defined as one who aspires to have a double bottom line. In other words, along with the pursuit of a positive financial bottom line would be the pursuit of another bottom line that supports some social cause. Observers often wonder if it is the financial bottom line that takes precedence over the social bottom line or just the reverse.

J. Gregory Dees, a researcher in this area, suggests that his research suggests the proposition that the social mission is the most important criterion to most social entrepreneurs. He believes that wealth, the financial bottom line, is a means to an end for most who follow a social mission.[18]

On the other hand, there are those researchers who look at social entrepreneurship along a continuum. At one extreme would be those social entrepreneurs who are driven solely by social benefits. At the other end of the spectrum would be social entrepreneurs who are driven by profitability with social benefits being the means to the end.[19]

THE FUTURE

In an interview with *Fortune* magazine, Neil Blumenthal in commenting on the disruptive nature of the Warby Parker model suggested, "The best businesses solve real problems. We've created an example of a business that can scale, be profitable, and do good in the world without charging a premium."[20]

What lies ahead for the company? One can only speculate about the uncharted waters that Gilboa and Blumenthal might explore.

NOTES

1. Warby Parker Business Model Toolbox. https://bmtoolbox.net/stories/warby-parker/. Accessed June 21, 2019.

2. Eng, Dinah (May 30, 2019). In hindsight: How Warby Parker got its start, *Fortune*. http://www.fortune.com/2019/05/30/warby-parker-founders/. Accessed August 1, 2019.

3. Ibid.

4. Building momentum in men's wear (April 5, 2012). *WWD*, 2b. *Academic OneFile*. http://link.galegroup.com/apps/doc/A286522382/AONE?u=txshracd2488&sid=AONE&xid=2f7f1c2d. Accessed July 15, 2019.

5. Chafkin, Max (February 17, 2015). Warby Parker sees the future of retailing. *Fast Company*. https://www.fastcompany.com/3041334/warby-parker-sees-the-future-of-retailing. Accessed July 15, 2019.

6. Ibid.

7. Chafkin, Max (February 17, 2015). Warby Parker sees the future of retailing. *Fast Company*. https://www.fastcompany.com/3041334/warby-parker-sees-the-futre-of-retailing. Accessed July 15, 2019.

8. Eng, Dinah (May 30, 2019). In hindsight: How Warby Parker got its start. *Fortune*. http://www.fortune.com/2019/05/30/warby-parker-founders/. Accessed August 1, 2019.

9. Girard, Keith (December 6, 2005). Small business borrowing strong. *Daily News Digest*. http://www.allbusiness.com/news/daily_news.asp?ID=11430#11431. Accessed August 18, 2019.

10. Chafkin, Max (February 17, 2015). Warby Parker sees the future of retailing. *Fast Company*. https://www.fastcompany.com/3041334/warby-parker-sees-the-future-of-retailing. Accessed July 15, 2019.

11. Eng, Dinah (May 30, 2019). In hindsight: How Warby Parker got its start. *Fortune*. http://www.fortune.com/2019/05/30/warby-parker-founders/. Accessed August 1, 2019.

12. Bazilian, Emma (April 22, 2013). *Adweek*, 54, No. 16, p. 20.

13. Grobant, Sam (August 12, 2013). Neil Blumenthal, co-CEO, co-founder Warby Parker. *Bloomberg Businessweek*, Issue 4342, p. 83.

14. IBISWorld (July 2019). Glasses & contact lens manufacturing in the U.S. https://www.Ibisworld.com. Accessed July 18, 2019.

15. Ibid.

16. Holgate, Mark (October 5, 2018). Warby Parker's latest collaboration not only benefits schoolkids, it will have you seeing stars. *Vogue*. https://www.yahoo.com/lifestyle/warby-parker-latest-collaboration-not-180000786.html. Accessed August 5, 2019.

17. Ibid.

18. Dees, J. Gregory (1998). Enterprising nonprofits. *Harvard Business Review*, 76, No. 1, 54-67.

19. Peredo, Ana Marie and Chrisman, James J. (2006). Social entrepreneurship: A critical review of the concept. *Journal of World Business*, 41, No. 1, 56–65.

20. Eng, Dinah (May 30, 2019). In hindsight: How Warby Parker got its start. *Fortune*. http://www.fortune.com/2019/05/30/warby-parker-founders/. Accessed August 1, 2019.

REFERENCES

Bazilian, Emma (April 22, 2013). *Adweek*, 54, No. 16, p. 20.

Building momentum in men's wear (April 5, 2012). *WWD*, 2b. *Academic OneFile*. https://link.galegroup.com/apps/doc/A286522382/AONE?u=txshracd2488&sid=AONE&xid=2f7f1c2d. Accessed July 15, 2019.

Chafkin, Max (February 17, 2015). Warby Parker sees the future of retailing. *Fast Company*. https://www.fastcompany.com/3041334/warby-parker-sees-the-future-of-retailing. Accessed July 15, 2019.

Dees, J. Gregory (1998). Enterprising nonprofits. *Harvard Business Review*, 76, No. 1, 54–67.

Eng, Dinah (May 30, 2019). In hindsight: How Warby Parker got its start. *Fortune*. http://www.fortune.com/2019/05/30/warby-parker-founders/. Accessed August 1, 2019.

Girard, Keith (December 6, 2005). Small business borrowing strong. *Daily News Digest*. http://www.allbusiness.com/news/daily_news.asp?ID=11430#11431. Accessed August 18, 2019.

Grobant, Sam (August 12, 2013). Neil Blumenthal, co-CEO, co-founder Warby Parker. *Bloomberg Businessweek*, Issue 4342, p. 83.

Holgate, Mark (October 5, 2018). Warby Parker's latest collaboration not only benefits schoolkids, it will have you seeing stars. *Vogue*. https://www.yahoo.com/lifestyle/warby-parker-latest-collaboration-not-180000786.html. Accessed August 5, 2019.

IBISWorld (July 2019). Glasses & contact lens manufacturing in the U.S. https://222.ibisworld.com. Accessed July 18, 2019.

Peredo, Ana Marie and Chrisman, James J. (2006). Social entrepreneurship: A critical review of the concept. *Journal of World Business*, 41, No. 1, 56–65.

Warby Parker Business Model Toolbox. https://bmtoolbox.net/stories/warby-parker/. Accessed June 21, 2019.

2

Entrepreneurial mindset – WeWork: can a shared space provider survive a recession?

http://www.wework.com

On Tuesday, August 20, 2019, the heading on an article in the *Waco Tribune-Herald* read "Most Surveyed Economists Predict Recession by 2021." The article beneath the heading read, in part:

> A strong majority, 74%, of U.S. business economists appear sufficiently concerned about the risks of some of President Trump's economic policies that they expect a recession in the U.S. by the end of 2021.[1]

Since the shared space provider, WeWork, was founded after the "Great Recession" of 2008–09, there was speculation by observers that a possible recession would create a serious problem for this company and other shared space companies.

BACKGROUND ON THE COMPANY

Mission

"Create a world where people work to make a life, not a living."

Founding

In 2010, shortly after the "Great Recession," Adam Neumann and Miguel McKelvey founded WeWork. Their intention with this startup was "…empowering creators to be more successful by leveraging the power of a global community. Together we've built a platform that allows our members to focus on growing their businesses, while we take care of everything else."[2]

The company bought buildings or two or three floors of buildings all over the world to provide shared spaces for startup or small businesses. In 2019, WeWork bought the iconic Lord & Taylor building in Manhattan through a joint venture which was called WeWork Property Investors. This Fifth Avenue landmark building was supposed to become the headquarters for WeWork. About that time, WeWork was valued at $47 billion.[3] However, by

October 6, 2019, the *New York Post* suggested that the building had become an albatross about the throat of the company. And as of that same month, WeWork was Manhattan's largest office tenant with over 5 million square feet.

On August 14, 2019, the company filed for an initial public offering (IPO) and revealed mounting losses as it attempted to scale its business and global locations. WeWork, which changed its name to the We Company, was attempting to raise $3 to $4 billion through the IPO to fund their future growth. For the six months which ended June 30, 2019, the company had reported revenue of $1.54 billion with a net loss of more than $900 million.[4]

Offerings

The company provided the following office spaces:

1. <u>Private office</u>. This included a private, enclosed, lockable office with all the benefits of membership, plus an added sense of privacy. Tenants were able to access their space 24/7. Membership benefits were the internet, cleaning, utilities, printing, mail and package handling and conference room credits. The offices were furnished with desks, lamps, chairs, and filing cabinets. (See the company website for pictures of all of their office offerings.)
2. <u>Dedicated desk</u>. The dedicated desk provided the worker with unlimited access to any available workspace in the location of the worker's choice. This also gave individuals access to their own workstations. This option included all membership benefits and conference room credits.
3. <u>Hot desk</u>. The hot desk gave the worker access to shared workspace and conference rooms in a WeWork building of the renter's choice.
4. <u>Lab desk</u>. With this arrangement, the worker could join a community of early-stage startups. Membership included desk space, membership and education.
5. <u>Membership</u>. This provision included access to all of WeWork's services and amenities and allowed the worker to book daily workspace and hourly meeting space in locations around the world. In addition, mail and package handling could be added at an additional cost.

Some other provisions of WeWork in addition to office space were: Lunch & Learn sessions allowing members to share expertise, knowledge and valuable tips; Office Hours which provided for one-on-one sessions with investors and industry leaders; Weekly Happy Hours and Networking Events.

A comparison of WeWork's prices and best features with other shared office space providers is outlined in Table 2.1.

The greatest benefit offered by shared office space providers was an economical alternative for startups, individual entrepreneurs, freelancers and businesses that would like to have satellite locations. It appeared that shared office space providers were moving into the arena of lower-cost offices formerly provided by business incubators. The primary difference was that business incubators only accepted completely new businesses that might need some assistance in surviving. However, the incubators did provide some of the same type of Lunch & Learn experiences that WeWork provided. Another commonality of business incubators with the

Table 2.1   Best shared office space summary table

Shared Office Space	Best For	Pricing From
WeWork	Coworking space and/or private office space	$575/month
Regus	The most locations in the industry	$330/month
LiquidSpace	Airbnb-like service, but for short-term office space, even hourly	$10/hour
Industrious	Another coworking and/or private office space option	$495/month
Servcorp	Virtual office space	$112/month
Davinci	Another virtual office space station	$50/month

Source: Graham, Gavin (January 8, 2018). Top 6 shared office space providers for 2018. *FitSmallBusiness.* https://fitsmallbusiness.com/shared-office-space-providers/. Accessed June 21, 2019.

Table 2.2   WeWork shared office space pricing

Number of Seats	Dedicated Desk	Private Office
One Seat	$575/month per desk	$810/month
Two Seats		$1,410/month
Three Seats		$2,000/month
Four Seats		$2,300/month
Five Seats		$2,800/month

Source: Graham, Gavin (January 8, 2018). Top 6 shared office space providers for 2018. *FitSmallBusiness.com.* https://fitsmallbusiness.com/shared-office-space-providers/. Accessed June 21, 2019.

shared space office providers was that both types of office spaces primarily attempted to use older space that was no longer available or useful for its original purpose.

Although individual pricing varied based on the location and type of workspace membership selected, Table 2.2 provides a rough guideline of WeWork prices.

By the fall of 2019, over 210,000 entrepreneurs, freelancers and creators were housed in WeWork workspaces. The company was located in over 400 locations worldwide in over 100 cities and provided a 25 percent reduction in typical office costs.

WORKPLACE OFFICE SPACE TRENDS

In the United States, office inventory represents over 12 billion square feet of space and $16 trillion in value.[5] The variables that influence the number of square feet per employee that is required by businesses are such things as workspace utilization levels, relative rent levels and cycles, tenant type, occupant turnover, firm growth rates and culture.[6]

Most corporate real estate managers allow approximately 100 square feet per worker for office space. Workspace allocation is usually much less in Asia and the more expensive

European markets. One reason that U.S. space per worker figures are so high is because so many firms last only a few years.

In addition to the usual work office spaces in buildings, by 2019 there was a trend toward alternative work environments such as distance working from home, coffee shops, libraries or "third workplaces." This allowed the sharing of workspaces in an office by several employees who might schedule their appearance at work in conjunction with other employees. This was called "office hoteling."

In a soft economy, one would expect the use of more "shadow space." This is space which is leased but is not occupied. Because labor costs are normally more expensive than office space, it often makes sense for a company to honor their leases until the lease expires and pay for more space than they need.[7]

In terms of space requirement by industry, law firms tend to lease more space with accounting firms, financial offices and other professional services coming in a close second. Another factor to consider in allocating space is the type of office space required. If a standardized office space will work for a company, the price of the space will be much lower. However, if there are differing requirements for office space, the amount of space demanded and the price of the space will go up. These varying space conditions give rise to the shared office space providers such as WeWork.

THE OFFICE LEASING INDUSTRY IN THE U.S.

The key economic drivers of the office leasing industry were the following: National unemployment rate, number of businesses, investor uncertainty, prime rate, corporate profit and office rental vacancy. The annual growth rate of the industry revenues from 2014 to 2019 was 1.9 percent. The office market was the main driver of demand for the Commercial Leasing Industry and accounted for 44.7 percent of industry revenues. Office leasing had also been one of the fastest-growing markets in that five-year period because of the employment expansion during the recovery from the "Great Recession" of 2008–09.

However, the predicted growth rate for industry revenues for the years 2019–24 was –0.6 percent. The reason for the predicted negative growth rate in revenues for those years was that as the U.S. economy stabilized and interest rates were expected to rise, industry operators were expected to be forced to adjust to fluctuating demand during this period. With expected increased unemployment over these five years, the incentive for companies to lease more office space to accommodate new workers was predicted to decrease. In addition, low growth in corporate profit and an increase in investor uncertainty would pose threats for leasing companies. This was because the unemployment rate was a major factor in determining the health of the U.S. economy.[8]

Although the industry revenue was $215.9 billion in 2018, the expected revenue outlook for the industry in the coming years is shown in Table 2.3.

Table 2.3 Revenue outlook for the commercial leasing industry, 2020–25

Year	Revenue in $ million	Growth %
2020	213,393.2	–1.2
2021	209,826.4	–1.7
2022	207,367.3	–1.2
2023	207,841.0	0.2
2024	209,084.5	0.6
2025	210,151.3	0.5

Source: IBISworld (March 2019). Commercial leasing in the U.S. IBISworld Industry Report 53112.

Because of the expectation of increased unemployment and a decrease in industry revenue, the industry is expected to become more conservative in terms of managing debt and leveraging assets. As a result of the "Great Recession" of 2008-09 initiated by the subprime mortgage crisis, companies are expected to try to maintain a strong balance sheet.[9]

THE GREAT RECESSION

Causes

The "Great Recession" was a global economic downturn that began in December 2007 and lasted through June of 2009. This crisis disrupted the financial markets and the real estate industry around the world. The initiation of the downfall began in February of 2007 when Freddie Mac (Federal Home Loan Mortgage Corporation) made an announcement that they would no longer buy the risky subprime mortgages and other mortgage-related securities. Then the subprime mortgage lender New Century Financial declared bankruptcy in April of 2007. Subsequently in August of that year, American Home Mortgage Investment Corporation declared Chapter 11 bankruptcy. Later in the summer, Standard & Poor's and Moody's credit rating services announced that they would reduce their ratings on more than 100 bonds backed by second lien subprime mortgages. After all of these events occurred, housing prices across the country began to fall causing many homeowners to be "under water" which meant that their homes were now valued less than their loan amounts.[10]

Outcomes

The "Great Recession" was the most severe downturn in the U.S. economy since the Great Depression of the late 1920s. The annual Gross Domestic Product (GDP) per capita growth was negative during 2008 and 2009.[11] The unemployment rate remained above 7 percent until 2014.[12] In addition, the median price of a house declined by 12.6 percent from 2007 to 2009. Each one of these events represented a negative shock to the American people.[13]

In 2007 and 2008, Wall Street experienced more tumultuous events than at any other time since 1929. When the credit markets and the stock market indices dropped, Barack Obama was elected president with the hope that he would be able to turn the economy around. Analysts had suggested that the lack of due diligence by investment bankers had helped create the market crash of 1929 and also would help with the push for financial reform in 2009. Insufficient collateral pledged against mortgage-backed securities was the culprit in both cases.[14]

Remedies

Several important remedies were initiated by the Federal Government in an attempt to pull the economy out of the trough of the business cycle. These initiatives were:

1. <u>Federal Reserve Board Drops Interest Rates</u>. This is a measurement that lenders use in deciding on rates they will use for loans. Interest rates had been at 5.25 percent in September of 2007; and by the end of 2008, the target rate had been reduced to zero.
2. <u>Stimulus Package</u>. In February of 2008, President George W. Bush signed into law the Economic Stimulus Act. This provided taxpayers with rebates of between $600 to $1,200. Taxes were also reduced, and the loan limit for federal home loan programs was reduced.[15]
3. <u>Troubled Asset Relief Program</u>. President Bush also approved this program which provided the government $700 billion to acquire the assets of troubled companies in order to keep them going.
4. <u>Dodd–Frank Act</u>. President Obama signed this act into law in 2010. It allowed the Federal Government to gain control of banks that were very weak and implement some customer protections to preserve their investments.

THE FUTURE

As 2020 quickly approached and a large percentage of business economists predicted a possible recession, the future of many small business owners looked precarious. The fact that the very definition of a recession is a negative GDP suggested that in a downturn of the economy many small businesses find it difficult to survive. Because businesses similar to WeWork made their real money in the private offices occupied by small businesses, not in the shared office or dedicated desk/hot desk, observers wondered how another recession might affect this segment of the commercial leasing industry.

NOTES

1. Gordon, March (August 20, 2019). Most surveyed economists predict recession by 2021. *Waco Tribune-Herald*, Business Section, p. 5A.
2. WeWork Brochure (n.d.). Our mission. https://www.wework.com/mission. Accessed June 21, 2019.
3. Boyte-White, Claire (August 14, 2019). How WeWork works and makes money. *Investopedia*. https://www.investopedia.com/articles/investing/082415/how-wework-works-and-makes-money.asp. Accessed August 22, 2019.

4. Ibid.

5. Florance, Andrew C., Miller, Norm G., Spivey, Jay and Peng, Ruijue (May 2010). Slicing, dicing and scoping the size of the U.S. commercial real estate market. *Journal of Real Estate Portfolio Management*, 16, No. 2, 111–128.

6. Miller, Norm G. (2014). Workplace trends in office space: Implications for future office demand. *Journal of Corporate Real Estate, Bingley*, 16, No. 3, 159–173.

7. Ibid.

8. IBISWorld (March 2019). Commercial leasing in the U.S. IBISWorld Industry Report 53112.

9. Ibid.

10. History.com Editors (August 21, 2018). Great Recession. https://www.history.com/topics/21st-century/recession/. Accessed August 20, 2019.

11. World Bank (2015). World development indicators. http://data.worldbank.org/data-catalog/world-development-indicators/. Accessed July 1, 2015.

12. U.S. Bureau of Labor Statistics (2015). Annual employment rate: Not seasonally adjusted for population 16 years and over. http://www.bls.gov/lau/#data/. Accessed July 1, 2015.

13. O'Connor, Kelsey (2017). Who suffered the most from the great recession? Happiness in the United States. *The Russell Sage Foundation Journal of the Social Sciences*, 3, No. 3, 72–99.

14. Geisst, Charles (Fall 2012). The great recession. *Financial History*. New York, Issue 104, pp. 36–39.

15. History.com Editors (August 21, 2018). Great Recession. https://www.history.com/topics/21st-century/recession. Accessed August 20, 2019.

REFERENCES

Boyte-White, Claire (August 14, 2019). How WeWork works and makes money. *Investopedia*. https://www.investopedia.com/articles/investing/082415/how-wework-works-and-makes-money.asp. Accessed August 22, 2019.

Florance, Andrew C., Miller, Norm G., Spivey, Jay and Peng, Ruijue (May 2010). Slicing, dicing and scoping the size of the U.S. commercial real estate market. *Journal of Real Estate Portfolio Management*, 16, No. 2, 111–128.

Geisst, Charles (Fall 2012). The great recession. *Financial History*. New York, Issue 104, pp. 36–39.

Gordon, March (August 20, 2019). Most surveyed economists predict recession by 2021. *Waco Tribune-Herald*, Business Section, p. 5A.

Graham, Gavin (January 8, 2018). Top 6 shared office space providers for 2018. *FitSmallBusiness*. https://fitsmallbusiness.com/shared-office-space-providers/. Accessed June 21, 2019.

History.com Editors (August 21, 2018). Great Recession. https://www.history.com/topics/21st-century/recession/. Accessed August 20, 2019.

IBISWorld (March 2019). Commercial leasing in the U.S. IBISWorld Industry Report 53112.

Miller, Norm G. (2014). Workplace trends in office space: Implications for future office demand. *Journal of Corporate Real Estate, Bingley*, 16, No. 3, 159–173.

O'Connor, Kelsey (2017). Who suffered the most from the great recession? Happiness in the United States. *The Russell Sage Foundation Journal of the Social Sciences*, 3, No. 3, 72–99.

U.S. Bureau of Labor Statistics (2015). Annual employment rate: Not seasonally adjusted for population 16 years and over. http://www.bls.gov/lau/#data/. Accessed July 1, 2015.

WeWork Brochure (n.d.). Our mission. https://www.wework.com/mission. Accessed June 21, 2019.

World Bank (2015). World development indicators. http://data.worldbank.org/data-catalog/world-development-indicators/. Accessed July 1, 2015.

3

Recognizing a good opportunity – White Trash Services: targeting a new market?

http://www.whitetrashservices.com

B.J. and Scott Nelson were sitting around the table in their small conference room doing some long-range planning. It was now the summer of 2020, and their trash service to rural home owners had been successful beyond their dreams. However, having saturated the six counties in Southwest Texas, they now wondered if they should begin to target larger towns and cities. The giant Waste Management company had concentrated on the cities and left the rural customers alone, and they pondered whether or not they could compete against the industry leader on their own playing field. They also knew they would need to calculate whether seeking such a larger market would even be worthwhile for them.

BACKGROUND ON THE NELSONS

Although B.J. had received an undergraduate degree in education from Baylor University, she decided not to become a teacher. Instead, she moved to Houston where her parents lived and began selling real estate. Toward the end of the several years that she sold real estate, she met her future husband, Scott, at church. Soon after that meeting, the two decided to get married. Their marriage took place in 1990, and it was not long before the first child came along. After that, two more children joined the family. B.J. decided to give up working outside and stay home with their three children.

Scott grew up in Katy, Texas, on a rice farm. He loved farming and decided to get a degree in agriculture from Texas A&M University where he was a Corps Cadet. While at the university, he dreamed of going back to Katy and being a rice farmer; but instead he took a job in a cattle feed lot owned by the Cargill Company in the Panhandle of Texas. He worked there for two years in a management training program and then moved to Houston. Then he began a career in industrial sales and stayed with this path for 25 years. It was while he was in Houston that he met and married B.J. In 1999, they moved to Victoria, Texas, where he continued his work in industrial sales. One problem they encountered was that he was often gone from home seeking sales and was missing some of the events that occurred while his children were growing up.

BACKGROUND ON WHITE TRASH SERVICES

In 2009, the only trash service that existed in most cities in Texas and the rest of the United States was the large Waste Management company and a couple of other large firms. The Nelsons had never thought much about trash services until one day when B.J. saw a B&B Trash Services truck, and she called and talked to the owner—a rather gruff man. She found out that their service was cheaper than any of the other services, and so the couple decided to use their service.

They could tell from the beginning that this was a very uncomplicated organization lacking the use of any of the more efficient tools most businesses utilized. For example, their bill came on a piece of paper with the amount of the service handwritten on it. B.J. recalled that the only checks she ever wrote were for this service and their church.

One day Scott was at home, and he saw the B&B Trash Services driver out front picking up their trash. He went out and talked with him, and the driver told Scott that the owner wanted to sell the business. Scott thought about presenting this opportunity to a friend, but B.J. convinced him that they should consider purchasing the business themselves. If they did, that would solve the problem of Scott being away from home so much with his sales job. He discovered that one of his high school friends had started a trash business with a truck and a trailer and later sold the business to BFI for $7 million. This made him think more seriously about this opportunity that had presented itself to them.

B.J. and Scott thought about this opportunity and prayed about it for a year. Scott's parents had friends in Houston who had a trash service; and when he asked for their advice about this opportunity, they encouraged him to pursue it. Finally in June of 2014, they bought the assets—not the company or the name—from the owner of B&B Trash Services. Scott had a cousin in Houston who had gone to an Ivy League school and then worked for a company in mergers and acquisitions for 20 years. He agreed to help them with the reorganization of the company.

Obtaining information from the former owner was very difficult. He never did produce any financial statements, but he finally said at the present time he was bringing in about $160,000 in revenue and had about $40,000 in net profit. He did not have a record of expenses, but he did have them in his head. From the things that the former owner was able to recall, Scott was able to come up with an income statement.

One day, B.J. came in and said, "We need to change the name of the business since we bought the assets but not the company and its name." Scott, being a wise cracker, said, "What about White Trash Services?" Everyone they ran this name by loved the idea. One of their friends said she would help with the logo, but she thought the name was offensive. B.J. and Scott asked a friend who was a radio host in Houston what he thought about the name, and he said he loved it. His comment was, "You're not going to please everyone, but most people will think the title is clever."

Operations

B.J. went to the Small Business Administration in Victoria to discuss the plan to run the business, and one man said, "You need to figure out what is different about your business." She thought that was a good idea. For one thing, they were cheaper than other services, but they did not want to push that because it might cause people to think their product was of lower quality. They decided the biggest advantage they had over Waste Management was that they were local; and when a customer called the local number, someone answered who knew the area well. When someone called Waste Management, they would get a person in Dallas or Phoenix who might not know anything about the area the company served.

The couple decided that they would focus on outstanding customer service in their dealings with their customers. The couple determined that when they said they would do something for someone, they would always do it as quickly as possible. They focused their advertisements on buying this service from a local company.

Their biggest fear when they began the service was that the customers the former owner said he had did not exist. He had told them when he sold the business that he had approximately 400 customers. He kept a notebook with their names in it along with the date they were billed and when they paid. An advantage of this kind of business, they found, was that you bill and collect on the service before the service is rendered and you have to pay your bills. That helped with cash flow. They got the books from the former owner in May, and they stayed up all night putting everything into QuickBooks. The White Pages were their biggest help. Scott ran the accounts receivable and gave a copy to the former owner. He found out that he was owed $10,000, and he did not know it.

In June of 2014, they bought the two trucks the former owner had and kept his two drivers. They had been running one truck two days a week and the other truck three days a week. Scott asked one of the drivers, "How do you know where you are going?" The driver answered that he had memorized the route. That frightened the Nelsons because they wondered what would happen if one of the drivers got sick or quit, and no one knew the route that had to be run. Therefore, B.J. took two of her children on different days to drive their car and follow the truck while she wrote down the route. Then she put all of this in GPS so that if a driver quit, they would know what the route was that he normally ran. There was actually software for this industry, but it was too expensive for them at the beginning of their business.

By the spring of 2020, they were operating in six counties of Texas: Victoria, Goliad, LaVaca, DeWitt, Jackson, and Calhoun. These were all located in the Southwest part of Texas.

Finances

The first year of operation, Scott kept his full-time job. They did not take anything out of the business that year. His cousin did the work for them for free to help the business get started, and then he continued his work by taking part ownership in the company.

When the Nelsons were talking to the former owner about the purchase of the assets, he asked them to pay for the company upfront. However, Scott suggested to him that it would be to his advantage for them to pay him over several years into the future. In that way, he would not be placed in a much higher tax bracket during the year of the purchase. The former owner agreed that this plan made sense, so they all agreed it would be purchased by owner financing. Scott had grown up on a farm where you are paid once a year when the crops come in, and he understood the tax implications of getting a large sum of money at one time.

The couple explained that they had been on an emotional roller-coaster since they purchased the business. They closed the deal at a title company, and they both felt as if they had jumped off a cliff since there were so many unknowns about the company. After they had been in business for a while, they went on a short cruise and wondered if the business would go under while they were gone.

At the time they bought the business, they were raising cattle; so they parked the trucks in the pasture and operated the business out of their home. They moved into a separate building where they could park their trucks in April of 2018. They had outgrown their home as a base of operations.

Assets in 2020

By the spring of 2020, the company had the following 14 trucks:
    7 rear-load trucks for residential;
    3 front-load trucks for dumpsters; and
    4 roll-off trucks for commercial.
They borrowed money for the additional trucks. However, they were able to finance part of the purchase through internal cash flow. They also bought 40 boxes which are big construction type containers. In May of 2018, they bought a roll-off truck company, and gained two trucks and 40 to 50 boxes. They bought 10 more immediately.

Residential trash service included picking up the container (see Figure 3.1 entitled "White Trash Services residential containers") once a week from a home site.

Dumpsters could be rented from White Trash whenever the home or organization had more trash than one or two trash cans, included a site where multiple families were living on a property sharing a trash service, or a business outside the city limits (see Figure 3.2 entitled "White Trash Services dumpster").

A 15-, 20-, 30- or 40-yard roll-off dumpster could be rented for either commercial businesses or residential applications. If a family or organization had to clean up after a major project, they could rent a dumpster that would fit their needs (see Figure 3.3 entitled "White Trash Services roll-off dumpster"). Whenever the dumpster was filled, the individual could call White Trash Services; and they would come and remove the dumpster.

Percentage of Business

By the spring of 2020, their percentage of business was the following:
    Residential was 60 percent. When they first took over the business it was 100 percent.
    Dumpsters represented 20 percent of the business.
    Roll-offs represented 20 percent of the business.

When they picked up commercial business, they had to have dumpsters and a truck to pick up dumpsters. They had a dumpster that had rusted out, and Scott wanted to rebuild it. However, a lady at a company he had dealt with said they were going to scrap some of their dumpsters, so Scott ended up buying 16 from her very inexpensively. Then they had to buy trucks to work with the dumpsters.

When they purchased the business, they were serving 90 percent outside Victoria County. During their analysis of the business, they projected 6,000 homes in Victoria County— excluding the city of Victoria. Six months into their operations, they started providing trash cans with their phone number and name on them. This was by far the most important way that they gained new business. They also had signs that were about the size of political campaign signs that they would stick in the ground in high impact areas. They had about 300 of these signs made, but they had a short life expectancy. They also began using billboards which were more expensive than any other marketing tool they used, but they were highly visible.

Only two times since they began the business had they not had any new customers in a week. When they were working from their home, they averaged 8 to 15 new customers a week. After they went into their building, they were averaging 10 to 25 new customers a week.

THE WASTE SERVICES INDUSTRY

The companies that operate in this industry collect waste from residential, industrial and commercial customers (see Table 3.1 entitled "Waste collection services products and services segmentation in 2018).

Table 3.1   Waste collection services products and services segmentation in 2018

Segment	Percentage of the Market
Residential Waste Collection	40.2
Non-Residential Waste Collection	22.3
Transfer and Storage Facility	7.8
Recyclable Material Collection	5.9
Collection and Demolition Waste Collection	2.8
Other	16.3

Source: IBISWorld (n.d.). Waste collection services in the U.S. in 2018, p. 4. www.ibisworld.com/was tecollectionservices. Accessed January 16, 2019.

This industry had a steady performance rate from 2013 through 2018. It had an annual growth rate of 1.7 percent to $48.7 billion through 2017.

From 2013 through 2018 the industry benefitted from rising industrial, construction and commercial business activity. In addition, there was a growing interest in solid waste recycling and renewable energy generation from solid waste. Companies in this industry have also benefitted from a growing trend among municipalities to privatize waste collection duties which they have historically provided on their own or outsourced.

Key Drivers of Demand

One of the drivers of demand in the industry is the growth in population in the United States. The Environmental Protection Agency suggested that in the years leading up to 2020, per capita generation of waste had been relatively stable. In addition, the population was expected to experience very little growth through 2020.[1]

Another driver of demand was the need for recycling facilities. This was a major source of industry demand. The processing of recyclable material was more expensive than most of the other industry services. The reason for this was that these materials had to be separated and sorted prior to their collection.

The construction sector was another driver of demand. This sector produced waste in the form of wood, concrete, rubble and other bulky refuse. When construction activity was high, the demand for waste services increased.

The manufacturing sector historically generated a large portion of the annual United States waste. Some of this waste was hazardous which was more expensive to collect. Normally, industrial waste was collected by private waste providers.

Another external factor that affected this industry was the price of diesel fuel. The reason for that was that most of the waste disposal trucks were powered by diesel fuel. The price of diesel and other fossil fuels was expected to increase.

Industry Trends

Government legislation and increasing public pressure for recycling have pushed for greater means of preparing for recycling and other means of waste diversion. This boded well for waste collection services because procedures for dealing with recyclables brought higher revenues than unsorted trash. In addition, waste services were able to sell the recyclables to recycling facilities instead of dumping the waste at a landfill.

As demand for waste services has grown, the number of providers for collection and disposal of waste has grown. However, IBISWorld expected the number of industry enterprises to increase modestly.[2] Despite the adoption of cost-saving waste collection methods, such as single driver trucks and automated optical sorting equipment, much of the industry work was still labor-intensive.

There has been a growing demand for landfills to be located further away from major population centers. This means that trucks had to drive further to reach the landfills, use more diesel fuel and decrease profit margins for the collection services.

One of the characteristics of a modern economy is the presence of waste collection and disposal. Since waste disposal is imperative for public health, waste collection services have existed since the time that people began to accumulate in cities. The industry in 2020 was characterized by well-defined service and market segments, continued consolidation and vertical integration, a low level of technological change and rising regulation.

WASTE MANAGEMENT COMPANY

This Houston-based company was the largest provider of integrated environmental solutions in North America. By 2020, they were serving more than 21 million municipal, commercial and industrial customers in the United States and Canada. In addition to providing waste disposal and recycling, they were engaged in personal counseling to help customers achieve their green goals including zero waste. The company also recovered the naturally occurring gas inside landfills to generate electricity. This operation was called "landfill-gas-to energy." Their fleet of natural gas trucks was the largest heavy-duty truck fleet of its kind in North America.

The company handled 15 million tons of recyclables in 2018. Their goal was to handle 20 million tons by the end of 2020. They also employed 43,000 full-time employees. Another related business the company had gotten into was portable restroom services under the Port-O-Let name, street and parking lot sweeping services and interests in oil and gas producing properties.

CONSIDERATIONS IN MUNICIPALITY BIDDING

Scott had discovered that the franchise fee to provide trash services to the city of Victoria was 15 percent. This was an exclusive contract for which the service provider agreed to pay the city 15 percent of every dollar that they collected. The profit margin he desired after all costs were considered should be in the 20–25 percent range. The bidding document from the city of Victoria was to have been out in March of 2020 but was delayed until summer because of the COVID-19 virus that disrupted many municipality processes.

Capital Equipment Needed	
Dumpster truck cost	$250,000 each
Roll-off truck cost	$160,000 each
Dumpsters	
2 yard	$470 each
3 yard	$550 each
4 yard	$630 each
6 yard	$810 each
8 yard	$985 each
Roll-offs	
20 yard	$4,290 each
30 yard	$4,655 each
40 yard	$5,400 each
Operating Cost Variables	
Average weight of dumpster trash	70 lbs./cubic yard
Average weight of roll-off container trash	300 lbs./cubic yard
Dump fees	$52.41/ton
Labor rate including taxes	$22.50/hr.
Fuel cost	$2.39/gallon
Maintenance	$10,000/truck/year
Insurance	$5,000/truck/year
Tires	$8,000 truck/year

Below is an accounting of the equipment and maintenance that Scott concluded would be required to service the city of Victoria contract.

THE DECISION

Scott got out his yellow legal pad and began to calculate how much it would cost him to handle the Victoria contract. He wondered if he would be able to gain the desired 20-25 percent profit range if he did win the contract. This was a big decision for the Nelsons, and they wanted to get it right. The bid had to be completed within a month, so time was of the essence.

Source: https://www.whitetrashservices.com.

Figure 3.1   White Trash Services residential containers

Source: https://www.whitetrashservices.com.

Figure 3.2   White Trash Services dumpster

Source: https://www.whitetrashservices.com.

Figure 3.3   White Trash Services roll-off dumpster

NOTES

1. IBISWorld (n.d.). Waste collection services in the U.S. in 2018. www.ibisworld.com/wastecollectionservices. Accessed January 16, 2019.
2. IBISWorld (n.d.). Waste collection services in the U.S. in 2018, p. 5. www.ibisworld.com/wastecollecti onservices. Accessed January 16, 2019.

REFERENCE

IBISWorld (n.d.). Waste collection services in the U.S. in 2018. www.ibisworld.com/wastecollecti onservices. Accessed January 16, 2019.

4

Planning for the long run – Rakuten: how long can rapid growth be sustained?

http://www.rakuten.com/

It was fall of 2019, and the management of Rakuten had just announced that the planned introduction of the company's new mobile service in Japan would be delayed until the spring of 2020. The company had grown so quickly since its founding in 1997 and had moved into so many different markets that some observers wondered if Rakuten could continue to move into new markets and countries as quickly in the future.

BACKGROUND ON RAKUTEN

Rakuten was founded in 1997 as a Japanese e-commerce and internet company and head-quartered in Tokyo. The company's B2B2C[1] platform became the largest e-commerce site in Japan and one of the largest in the world by sales. The founder of the company was Hiroshi Mikitani who was educated at Harvard and was a former banker. His idea was to establish an online shopping mall that gave shoppers cash back on every purchase at a member merchant's site. The percentage of the cash back was established by each merchant. The company would also allow merchants the ability to control the design of their storefronts on the Rakuten site. In addition, Rakuten charged a smaller fee to merchants who partnered with them rather than other online shopping sites.

When the company was launched, it had six employees and 13 merchants paying a fee to be on the site. By 2020, Rakuten employed 10,000 people worldwide.

OFFERINGS TO MERCHANTS

Rakuten offered online merchants the following services:

1. Home page placements viewed by millions of visitors each month;
2. Participation opportunities in Rakuten's Cash Back promotions;
3. Enhanced visibility within their mobile app;
4. Increased exposure for their offers and promotions;

5. Inclusion in their weekly emails to 12 million members; and
6. Targeted email and Cash Back campaigns.

The Rakuten Rewards CEO, Amit Patel, said of the company's operations and their desire to hire creative people, "We're a team of innovators at the cutting edge of technology and marketing. If you're inspired to do work that pushes boundaries, we'd love to hear from you."[2]

PUBLIC OFFERINGS

Rakuten launched an Initial Public Offering on April 19, 2000. By this time, the company's online marketplace had 2,300 stores and had become one of the most popular sites in Japan.

ADDITIONAL ACQUISITIONS AND LAUNCHES

In March of 2001, their online hotel reservation service named Rakuten Travel was launched. The company also began offering a credit card in 2005. By November of 2016, their credit card was held by over 13 million people, and almost 40 percent of Rakuten's revenue was from financial services including the credit card and their internet bank.[3]

In 2008, Rakuten and President Chain Store established the company's first e-commerce site outside Japan in Taiwan.[4] The company was named Taiwan Rakuten Ichiba.

E-book retailer Kobo was purchased by Rakuten for $135 million in November of 2011. The company's head of Global Business, Kentaro Hyakuno, said that the intention of the company was to win market share in the book industry. He suggested

> We are working with SMEs (small and medium-sized business enterprises) in the United Kingdom and expanding our marketplace so that we are going to provide a platform to many UK SMEs, as well as on the Kobo site where we want to empower and work with booksellers and publishers to make sure they have the opportunity to grow with us.[5]

By 2018, Rakuten Kobo had become the second largest manufacturer of e-reading devices and accessories in the world. The company had added audiobooks to their portfolio in September of that year. The company had studied e-readers and their habits, and they discovered the following:

1. Their primary customers were middle-aged adults and retired people;
2. Their market segment liked the company's e-reader because they could change the font size to fit their individual needs and the product was lighter than other e-books; and
3. They also liked the fact that the e-books were waterproof and had adjustable lighting.

The company sold a selection of 5 million e-books and audiobooks in more than 100 languages and 150 countries. Rakuten Kobo was also working on reverse logistics which would involve analyzing customer return data to discover areas for improvement.[6]

The company began aggressively moving its operations outside Japan, and by 2012 Rakuten had online retail businesses in Austria, Canada, Spain, Taiwan, and Thailand. They also had online travel markets in France with Voyager Moins Cher.com. Then they launched their Rakuten Travel platform in China, Hong Kong, Korea, and Taiwan. In order to better connect with non-Japanese speakers, in 2012 the company adopted English as their official language.[7]

In 2014, the company purchased the U.S. shopping site Ebates and changed the name of the site to Rakuten which was pronounced RACK-uh-ten and was the Japanese word for "optimism." The reason for the change of the company's name was so that they might join forces with Rakuten which was a global leader in many areas. The Ebates site did not change. There was simply a new name and new logo. By 2020, the company paid out $1 billion to the 10 million members and had a Better Business Bureau (BBB) rating of A+.

In 2016, the company introduced Rakuten Pay which was an app-based smartphone payment system.[8]

In April 2017, the company formed a partnership with a California company named Blackstorm Labs to launch an online social gaming platform named R Games. The site went live with 15 free games for smartphones. The free games included Pac-Man and Space Invaders.[9]

In 2018, Rakuten announced that the company was set to make a splash in Japan's mobile phone market which for years had been dominated by three major companies.[10] However, by August of that year, the company announced that they were behind schedule on installing wireless base stations which would cause them to limit the scope of services at their October launch.[11] Later the company announced that they would delay the start of full mobile service until the spring of 2020.[12]

ALLIANCE WITH WALMART

In February of 2018, Rakuten announced it was launching a new online grocery delivery service in Japan beginning in the third quarter of the year. In addition to this move, Rakuten Kobo and Walmart rolled out an exclusive retail alliance in which Walmart would begin selling e-books, audiobooks and Rakuten Kobo e-readers in Walmart stores and online at Walmart.com in the United States later in the year.

Rakuten Chairman, President and CEO, Hiroshi "Mickey" Mikitani said of the deal, "As global leaders in e-commerce and offline shopping, Rakuten and Walmart are uniquely positioned to partner our customers around the world with innovative services. We are excited to partner with Walmart because of its commitment to creating the best solutions to serve customers with low prices."[13]

SPORTS INVESTMENTS

In October of 2004, Rakuten Baseball was launched. The Tohoku Rakuten Golden Eagles was formed in the Nippon Professional Baseball League.

Rakuten's first venture into the football arena was on November 16, 2016, when the company announced that it had entered into a four-year partnership with the La Liga football club in Barcelona. This team had been one of the most successful clubs in Europe. The partnership made Rakuten the main global partner beginning with the 2017-18 season. The deal was worth 220 million euros.[14]

Then in September of 2017, Rakuten signed a three-year $60 million deal which made the company the official sponsor for the jersey patch on the uniforms for the Golden State Warriors of the National Basketball Association.[15] In August of 2019, Rakuten entered into a broadcasting contract with the National Basketball Association in the State of Idaho.[16] Then in September of 2019, Rakuten reached an agreement to buy the popular Taiwanese pro baseball team Lamigo Monkeys. The company wanted to enter the league in time for the next season.

COLLECTING CUSTOMER DATA

Rakuten Marketing, which had become the global leader in omnichannel marketing by 2015, leveraged Krux's next-generation data management platform (DMP) to improve its consumer data for more personalized omnichannel marketing. The purpose of this move was to drive more meaningful experiences for consumers while it also enhanced advertisers' marketing strategies.

The purpose of Krux DMP was to unify people data from several of Rakuten's business sources and activate the data across multiple channels for targeted marketing campaigns. Rakuten Marketing CEO Tony Zito suggested:

Our mission is to empower advertisers to engage customers with more relevant and more impactful experiences—what we call the omni experience. Leveraging rich consumer data across Rakuten plays a big role in making that mission a reality. Krux is a best-in-class partner for its global leadership in data management and its track record of delivering demonstrative marketing ROI.[17]

Then in May of 2018, Rakuten released a white paper intended to educate advertisers and marketers on potential business implications of the General Data Protection Regulation (GDPR). (See Box 4.1 entitled "General Data Protection Regulation.") The document provided specific recommendations to help brands ensure compliance with the May 25 GDPR deadline.

Rakuten Marketing President Stuart Simms indicated:

Data protection is a critically important topic within our industry. The GDPR, although primarily affecting businesses in or working internationally within the European Union, brings global awareness of the importance of properly collecting and processing consumer data.[18]

SHOPPING SECRETS SURVEY

In late 2014, Rakuten conducted a survey with consumers over seven worldwide markets and found the following:

1. Americans would spend almost 14 hours shopping for friends and family that year.
2. The most difficult person to buy gifts for was a spouse or partner.
3. Spouses and partners, however, suggested that they would prefer hugs and kisses (43 percent); fashion accessories (29 percent); jewelry (27 percent); food (26 percent); or would love a blank check to pay their bills (13 percent).
4. When receiving an unwanted gift, respondents admitted to regifting the present to someone else (35 percent); donating it to charity (27 percent); or selling it off (14 percent).
5. More than half of the Americans surveyed dreaded going to the mall which is higher than their European or Asian counterparts.[19]

PROBLEMS FOR THE COMPANY

In Japan, Rakuten had become an Amazon.com lookalike. The company had expanded into sports, financial services and even family planning. When the company's baseball or soccer teams won a game, the 11 million credit card holders got extra points for purchases on its primary online marketplace, Ichiba. Hiroshi Mikitani, stated: "We invented this marketplace model, and our intentional competitors basically followed."[20]

However, outside of Japan, Rakuten did not have a recognizable name. Few people in the United States and Europe were even aware of the company. In those countries, Amazon was the major player and Alibaba was larger than the company in China.

Another concern for the company occurred in March 2014 when the U.K.-based Environmental Investigation Agency (EIA) named Rakuten as the world's biggest online retailer of whale meat and elephant ivory sales on its sites. The next month, Rakuten announced it was ending all online sales of whale and dolphin meat by the end of the month.[21] And in July of 2017, Rakuten announced that it was banning ivory sales on its sites.[22]

Then in 2016, Rakuten was forced to shut down retailing websites in the U.K., Spain, Austria, Singapore, Indonesia, and Malaysia.[23] Instead of expanding, Rakuten was actually retreating in these countries. Their stated strategy in doing this was to consolidate some of their retailing sites and focus on France and Germany where its websites had the scale and potential for sustainable growth.

JAPAN'S DECLINING ECONOMY

In the third quarter of 2018, Japan's economy shrunk the most that it had in the past four years. Along with that decline, Japanese companies cut their spending to weather the slowing global growth and trade problems.[24]

Japan's gross domestic product (GDP) shrunk at an annualized rate of 2.5 percent in that quarter. The decline was the result of a series of natural disasters that caused factories to cut production, which was the biggest decrease since the third quarter of 2009 during the worldwide "Great Recession." Consumption by households, which amounted to 60 percent of GDP, fell 0.2 percent in the third quarter. The capital expenditure part of GDP fell 2.8 percent from the second quarter, and this was the biggest decrease since the third quarter of 2009. This drop was attributed to a decline in spending by wholesalers, retailers and information and communications machinery manufacturers.[25] Many Japanese companies were also being affected by the United States–China trade controversy.

JAPAN'S DECLINING POPULATION

Japan's Health Ministry announced in 2018 that only 946,060 babies were born in Japan in 2017 which was the fewest births since 1899 when the country began collecting such statistics.[26] The Japanese population had grown steadily throughout the 20th century to 128 million in 2000. However, birth rates declined drastically from 2.1 children in the 1970s to 1.4 in 2018. Japan by 2015 had the oldest median age of any large country in the world (see Table 4.1 entitled "The oldest countries by median age, 2015").

Table 4.1   The oldest countries by median age, 2015

Ranking	Country	Median Age
1	Japan	46.3
2	Italy	45.9
3	Germany	45.9
4	Portugal	43.9
5	Martinique	43.7
6	Bulgaria	43.5
7	Greece	43.3
8	Austria	43.2
9	Hong Kong	43.2
10	Spain	43.2

Source: Kopf, Dan (June 4, 2018). The world is running out of Japanese people. *Quartz.* https://qz.com/1295721/the-japanese-population-is-shrinking-faster-than-every-other-big-country/. Accessed November 25, 2019.

Demographers believed there would be a drastic fall in population in Japan within the 21st century. They estimated that the Japanese population would fall to just over 100 million people by 2050 from 127 million in 2018.[27]

THE FUTURE

In view of the fact that Japan had a declining population and an economy that had slowed down considerably, Rakuten had to look to the future and determine the best way to proceed (see Table 4.2 entitled "Consolidated financial position of Rakuten"). In 2016, the country had to close down its retailing websites in the U.K., Spain, Austria, Singapore, Indonesia, and Malaysia which did not bode well for expansion into other countries. The management of the company had to look to the future and come up with a revised strategy.

BOX 4.1   GENERAL DATA PROTECTION REGULATION

The purpose of the General Data Protection Regulation (GDPR) was to standardize data protection laws across all 28 European Union countries. The act also imposed strict rules on controlling and processing identifiable information and extended protection of personal data by giving control to EU citizens.

The act replaced the 1995 EU Data Protection Directive and went into force on May 25, 2018. The regulation provided for increased fines, breach notifications, opt-in consent and responsibility for data transfer outside of the EU. This act permanently changed the way customer data was collected, stored and used.

GDPR applied to all organizations that held and processed EU residents' personal data. The fines for noncompliance could be as high as 20 million euros. The maximum fine could be imposed for the most serious violations such as not having sufficient customer consent to process data.[28]

Table 4.2   Consolidated financial position of Rakuten, December 31, 2017, to December 31, 2018 (conversion rate of $1 = 109 yen)

	December 31, 2018	December 31, 2017
Revenue	$10,105,000,000	$8,664,000,000
Operating Income	1,563,000,000	1,370,000,000
Net Income	1,301,000,000	1,013,000,000
Earnings per share attributable to owners of the company	$.96	$.73
Return on Equity	19.5%	16.2%
Return on Assets	2.4%	2.6%
Total Assets	67,385,000,000	56,736,000,000
Total Equity	7,121,000,000	6,269,000,000
Net Cash Flows from Operating Activities	1,335,000,000	1,486,000,000
Net Cash Flows from Investing Activities	(619,000,000)	(1,868,000,000)
Net Cash Flows from Financing Activities	208,000,000	1,784,000,000

Source: Rakuten website Financial Data.

NOTES

1. Business to business to consumer.

2. Rakuten website. https://www.rakuten.com/careers/. Accessed September 25, 2019.

3. Martin, Alexander and Mochizuki, Takashi (November 10, 2016). Rakuten banks on credit-card business growth. *The Wall Street Journal*. https://www.wsj.com/articles/rakuten-relies-on-credit-card-business-to-counter-slower-growth-1478779829/. Accessed November 10, 2019.

4. Wee, Willis (June 13, 2011). The history of Rakuten, Japan's largest e-commerce site. *Tech in Asia*. https://www.techinasia.com/rakuten-infographic/. Accessed October 3, 2019.

5. Campbell, Lisa (February 3, 2012). Kobo to grow at speed under Rakuten: Head of global business at Rakuten gives first UK interview to The Bookseller. *The Bookseller*. https://link.gale.com/apps/doc/A281588206/AONE?u=txshracd2488&sid=AONE&xid=fb5a6aab/. Accessed October 3, 2019.

6. Zeman, Kat (January 1, 2018). Listen up: Rakuten Kobo experiences steady growth and introduces audiobooks to its product portfolio. *Retail Merchandiser*, 58, No. 1, p. 94.

7. Haggin, Patience (October 2, 2016). Why a Japanese e-tailer requires workers to speak English. *The Wall Street Journal*. https://www.wsj.com/articles/why-a-japanese-e-tailer-requires-workers-to-speak-english-1475460061/. Accessed September 20, 2019.

8. Ibid.

9. Rakuten wants to disrupt the App Store (April 5, 2017). *Business Insider*. http://www.businessinsider.com/rakuten-wants-to-disrupt-the-app-store-2017-4. Accessed October 3, 2019.

10. Satake, Minoru (April 17, 2018). Rakuten's integrated services to prize open Japan's mobile market. *Nikkei Asia Review*. https://asia.nikkei.com/Business/Companies/Rakuten-s-integrated-services-to-prize-open-Japan-mobile-market/. Accessed October 2, 2019.

11. Ebuchi, Tomohiro (August 15, 2018). Rakuten's mobile network faces delays ahead of October launch. *Nikkei Asia Review*. https://asia.nikkei.com/Business/Telecommunication/Rakuten-s-mobile-network-faces-delays-ahead-of-October-launch/. Accessed October 3, 2019.

12. Hiroi, Yoichiro (September 6, 2019). Rakuten to delay Japan's newest mobile network by 6 months. *Nikkei Asia Review*. https://asia.nikkei.com/. Accessed October 30, 2019.

13. Walmart and Rakuten highlight new strategic alliance (February 2018). *Professional Services Closeup*. https://link.gale.com/apps/doc/A526305069/GPS?u=txshracd2488&sid=GPS&xid=f93fc118. Accessed October 3, 2019.

14. Rakuten ups its brand game with 220 million euro Barcelona sponsorship (November 16, 2016). *Financial Times*. https://www.ft.com/content/8873d0ca-ac1a-11e6-9cb3-bb8207902122?mhg5;=e3/. Accessed October 2, 2019.

15. Rovell, Darren (September 12, 2017). Warriors sign jersey-patch advertising deal with Rakuten. *ESPN*. https://www.espn.com/nba/story/-/id/20680169/golden-state-warriors-sign-jersey-patch-advertising-deal-rakuten/. Accessed October 2, 2019.

16. Suzuki, Masato (August 31, 2019). NBA deal poised to pay off for Japan's Rakuten after fast break. *Nikkei Asian Review*. https://asia.nikkei.com/Business/Media-Entertainment/NBA-deal-poised-to-pay-off-for-Japan-s-Rakuten-after-fast-break/. Accessed October 3, 2019.

17. Rakuten marketing activates data with Krux to improve consumer experiences (July 11, 2015). *Marketing Weekly News*, p. 58. https://link.gale.com/apps/doc/A420548467/GPS?u=txshracd2488&sid=GPS&xid=9aa2fb25. Accessed October 3, 2019.

18. Rakuten marketing releases white paper on global data protection regulation (May 3, 2018). *Wireless*. https://link.gale.com/apps/doc/A537112418/ITBC?u=txshracd2488&sid=ITBC&xid=d54bf1ba. Accessed October 3, 2019.

19. Rakuten showcases shopping secrets survey results (November 29, 2014). *Professional Services Close-Up*. https://link.gale.com/apps/doc/A391887248/GPS?u=txshracd2488&sid=GPS&xid=4f382367/.   Accessed October 3, 2019.

20. Einhorn, Bruce (April 13, 2015). Japan's Amazon has bigger dreams. *Bloomberg Businessweek*, Issue 4422.

21. McCurry, Justin (April 4, 2014). Japan's biggest online retailer, Rakuten, ends whale meat sales. https://www.theguardian.com/environment/2014/apr/04/rakuten-ends-whale-meat-sales/. Accessed October 20, 2019.

22. Japan's Rakuten retail site bans ivory sales (July 7, 2017). *BBC News*. https://www.bbc.com/news/world-asia-40535801/. Accessed October 20, 2019.

23. Martin, Alexander and Mochizuki, Takashi (November 10, 2016). Rakuten banks on credit-card business growth. *The Wall Street Journal*. https://www.wsj.com/articles/rakuten-relies-on-credit-card-business-to-counter-slower-growth-1478779829/. Accessed November 10, 2019.

24. Kajimoto, Tetsushi (December 9, 2018). Japan's economy shrinks most in four years as global risks hit business spending. *Business News*. https://www.reuters.com/article/us-japan-economy-gdp/japans-economy-shrinks-most-in-four-years-as-global-risks-hit-business-spending-idUSKBN/. Accessed November 25, 2019.

25. Ibid.

26. Kopf, Dan (June 4, 2018). The world is running out of Japanese people. *Quartz*. https://qz.com/1295721/the-japanese-population-is-shrinking-faster-than-every-other-big-country/. Accessed November 25, 2019.

27. Ibid.

28. Lahiti, Kris (February 14, 2018). What is General Data Protection Regulation? *Forbes*. https://www.forbes.com/sites/quora/2018/02/14/what-is-general-data-protection-regulation/#3e69d7f462dd/. Accessed November 25, 2019.

REFERENCES

Campbell, Lisa (February 3, 2012). Kobo to grow at speed under Rakuten: Head of global business at Rakuten gives first UK interview to The Bookseller. *The Bookseller*. https://link.gale.com/apps/doc/A281588206/AONE?u=txshracd2488&sid=AONE&xid=fb5a6aab/. Accessed October 3, 2019.

Ebuchi, Tomohiro (August 15, 2018). Rakuten's mobile network faces delays ahead of October launch. *Nikkei Asia Review*. https://asia.nikkei.com/Business/Telecommunication/Rakuten-s-mobile-network-faces-delays-ahead-of-October-launch/. Accessed October 3, 2019.

Einhorn, Bruce (April 13, 2015). Japan's Amazon has bigger dreams. *Bloomberg Businessweek*, Issue 4422.

Haggin, Patience (October 2, 2016). Why a Japanese e-tailer requires workers to speak English. *The Wall Street Journal*. https://www.wsj.com/articles/why-a-japanese-e-tailer-requires-workers-to-speak-english-1475460061/. Accessed September 20, 2019.

Hiroi, Yoichiro (September 6, 2019). Rakuten to delay Japan's newest mobile network by 6 months. *Nikkei Asia Review*. https://asia.nikkei.com/. Accessed October 30, 2019.

Japan's Rakuten retail site bans ivory sales (July 7. 2017). *BBC News*. https://www.bbc.com/news/world-asia-40535801/. Accessed October 20, 2019.

Kajimoto, Tetsushi (December 9, 2018). Japan's economy shrinks most in four years as global risks hit business spending. *Business News*. https://www.reuters.com/article/us-japan-economy-gdp/japans-economy-shrinks-most-in-four-years-as-global-risks-hit-business-spending-idUSKBN/. Accessed November 25, 2019.

Kopf, Dan (June 4, 2018). The world is running out of Japanese people. *Quartz.* https://qz.com/1295721/the-japanese-population-is-shrinking-faster-than-every-other-big-country/. Accessed November 25, 2019.

Lahiti, Kris (February 14, 2018). What is General Data Protection Regulation? *Forbes.* https://www.forbes.com/sites/quora/2018/02/14/what-is-general-data-protection-regulation/#3e69d7f462dd/. Accessed November 25, 2019.

Martin, Alexander and Mochizuki, Takashi (November 10, 2016). Rakuten banks on credit-card business growth. *The Wall Street Journal.* https://www.wsj.com/articles/rakuten-relies-on-credit-card-business-to-counter-slower-growth-1478779829/. Accessed November 10, 2019.

McCurry, Justin (April 4, 2014). Japan's biggest online retailer, Rakuten, ends whale meat sales. https://www.theguardian.com/environment/2014/apr/04/rakuten-ends-whale-meat-sales/. Accessed October 20, 2019.

Rakuten marketing activates data with Krux to improve consumer experiences (July 11, 2015). *Marketing Weekly News*, p. 58. https://link.gale.com/apps/doc/A420548467/GPS?u=txshracd2488&sid=GPS&xid=9aa2fb25. Accessed October 3, 2019.

Rakuten marketing releases white paper on global data protection regulation (May 3, 2018). *Wireless.* https://link.gale.com/apps/doc/A537112418/ITBC?u=txshracd2488&sid=ITBC&xid=d54bf1ba. Accessed October 3, 2019.

Rakuten showcases shopping secrets survey results (November 29, 2014). *Professional Services Close-Up.* https://link.gale.com/apps/doc/A391887248/GPS?u=txshracd2488&sid=GPS&xid=4f382367/. Accessed October 3, 2019.

Rakuten ups its brand game with 220 million euro Barcelona sponsorship (November 16, 2016). *Financial Times.* https://www.ft.com/content/8873d0ca-ac1a-11e6-9cb3-bb8207902122?mhg5;=e3/. Accessed October 2, 2019.

Rakuten wants to disrupt the App Store (April 5, 2017). *Business Insider.* http://www.businessinsider.com/rakuten-wants-to-disrupt-the-app-store-2017-4. Accessed October 3, 2019.

Rakuten website. https://www.rakuten.com/careers/. Accessed September 25, 2019.

Rovell, Darren (September 12, 2017). Warriors sign jersey-patch advertising deal with Rakuten. *ESPN.* https://www.espn.com/nba/story/-/id/20680169/golden-state-warriors-sign-jersey-patch-advertising-deal-rakuten/. Accessed October 2, 2019.

Satake, Minoru (April 17, 2018). Rakuten's integrated services to prize open Japan's mobile market. *Nikkei Asia Review.* https://asia.nikkei.com/Business/Companies/Rakuten-s-integrated-services-to-prize-open-Japan-mobile-market/. Accessed October 2, 2019.

Suzuki, Masato (August 31, 2019). NBA deal poised to pay off for Japan's Rakuten after fast break. *Nikkei Asian Review.* https://asia.nikkei.com/Business/Media-Entertainment/NBA-deal-poised-to-pay-off-for-Japan-s-Rakuten-after-fast-break/. Accessed October 3, 2019.

Walmart and Rakuten highlight new strategic alliance (February 2018). *Professional Services Closeup.* https://link.gale.com/apps/doc/A526305069/GPS?u=txshracd2488&sid=GPS&xid=f93fc118. Accessed October 3, 2019.

Wee, Willis (June 13, 2011). The history of Rakuten, Japan's largest e-commerce site. *Tech in Asia.* https://www.techinasia.com/rakuten-infographic/. Accessed October 3, 2019.

Zeman, Kat (January 1, 2018). Listen up: Rakuten Kobo experiences steady growth and introduces audiobooks to its product portfolio. *Retail Merchandiser*, 58, No. 1, p. 94.

5
Securing funding – Kickstarter: creating a platform for crowdfunding dreams

http://www.kickstarter.com

Kickstarter is one of those platforms that gives you space to work with people who know you, love you and support you.[1] (De La Soul)

This hip-hop trio from Amityville, Long Island, New York, announced early in 2015 that they would seek Kickstarter funding for their new album "And the Anonymous Nobody," and subsequently the project was funded and released on August 26, 2016. Kickstarter had been a very successful crowdfunding platform for them. However, by the spring of 2020, the larger number of unsuccessful projects on Kickstarter raised the question of the usefulness of spending, time, money, and energy on a platform that had such a high failure rate.

BACKGROUND ON KICKSTARTER

The idea for Kickstarter came from a failed project by Perry Chen, one of its founders. Chen was living in New Orleans in 2001 and wanted to bring a couple of disc jockeys down to the 2002 Jazz Fest. He found a perfect venue for the event, but the management of the venue asked for more money than he could raise. Something that troubled him about that failure was that the potential audience did not have any input into the decision. He began pondering ways that he could make that happen. Chen moved to New York City in 2005 and looked around for someone to build the website that might be needed to allow fans of an idea to put money into its creation.

Soon after arriving in New York, he met Yancey Strickler, and they bought a whiteboard and began brainstorming. Then a year later, Chen met Charles Adler, and the two of them began working on the specifications for the site. By the summer of 2008, Chen was introduced to Andy Baio who found developers for the site. On April 28, 2009, they launched Kickstarter to the public.[2]

Some of the early projects funded on Kickstarter were: Designing Obama, Robin Writes a Book and Mysterious Letters. Artists, writers, filmmakers, musicians, inventors, and game designers all put their ideas out for potential funding on the site.

MISSION

We built Kickstarter to help bring creative projects to life. We measure our success as a company by how well we achieve that mission, not by the size of our profits.

OUR COMMUNITY

Kickstarter is an enormous global community built around creativity and creative projects. Over 18 million people, from every continent on earth, have backed a Kickstarter project.

Some of these projects come from influential artists like De La Soul or Marina Abramovic. Most come from amazing creative people you probably haven't heard of—from Grandma Pearl to indie filmmakers to the band down the street.

HOW IT WORKS

In 2015, Kickstarter amended their charter to become a Benefit Corporation. This type of organization is a for-profit that must consider the impact of their decision on society—not only on shareholders.

Each project on Kickstarter is independently created and crafted by one or more potential entrepreneurs. They have complete control over their own projects and spend a great deal of time building the project pages, shooting their videos and determining what reward they will give to their backers. Each creator sets the project funding goal and the deadline for raising the funds. Once the project is up on Kickstarter, people who like the idea pledge funding with a credit card. If the project does succeed in reaching its funding goal, the credit cards are charged for the amount of the pledge. If the project does not meet its funding goal by the time of the deadline, the backers' cards are not charged.[3]

Unlike venture capital, funders of Kickstarter projects do not get an equity position in the business (see Figure 5.1 entitled "Funding sources for each venture stage.") However, they may get some type of reward such as the item funded itself. Since there is no possibility of becoming a part owner of the company, the reason people put their money into a Kickstarter project is that they love the idea, the creator or they are just supporting a friend's project. The reality is that the funders often get a psychic reward from investing in someone's dream. Kickstarter does not allow projects that are for a charity or offer financial incentives. In addition, Kickstarter does not guarantee projects or the creator's ability to complete the project. Kickstarter makes money by assessing a 5 percent fee on the funds raised on successfully funded projects. Those projects that are not funded are not charged a fee.

SUCCESSFULLY FUNDED PROJECTS

A total of $4,984,289,377 had been pledged to Kickstarter projects by May of 2020. That represented 182,018 successfully funded projects. The management of Kickstarter had discovered that most of the successfully funded projects raised less than $10,000, but some projects had reached 6, 7 or 8 figures. A breakdown of the projects presented on Kickstarter is shown in Table 5.1.

Table 5.1   Successful and unsuccessful projects

Successful Projects	Less than $1,000 raised	$1,000– $9,999 raised	$10,000– $19,999 raised	$20,000– $99,999 raised	$100,000– $999,999 raised	
182,018	23,753	98,453	26,163	26,590	6,614	

Unsuccessful Projects	0% funded	1–20% funded	21–40% funded	41–60% funded	61–80% funded	81–99% funded
300,962	55,588	193,797	30,254	12,562	5,092	3,662

Source: Kickstarter website. https://www.kickstarter.com/stats/. Accessed May 20, 2020.

Interestingly, more projects had failed than had been successfully funded. Some of the projects that were successfully funded and achieved some measure of success as a business were:

13 Kickstarter-funded films had been nominated for Academy Awards;

One film, *Inocente*, won an Oscar in 2013;

Kickstarter-funded albums had topped Billboard charts and won Grammys;

Artwork had been exhibited at MoMA, the Whitney Biennial, the Kennedy Center, the Walker Art Center, the Smithsonian and the American Folk-Art Museum;

Dances had been performed by the Martha Graham Dance Company;

New inventions had been adopted by tech giants.[4]

In 2013, the Pebble smartwatch gained $10.3 million in funding on Kickstarter and set a new record. Then later an ice chest named the Coolest Cooler with a USB-enabled Bluetooth speaker-pumping, illuminated, partitioned, accessory-holding cooler featuring an onboard blender topped the funding mark by raising over $11 million. The Portland-based creator named Ryan Grepper had only set a funding goal of $50,000.[5]

However, Grepper failed to reach his funding goal the first time he submitted his product on Kickstarter. He only raised $102,188 against a goal of $125,000 in his 2013 attempt. From this failure, Grepper decided he needed a better design, so he went back to the drawing board before submitting to Kickstarter the second time. In discussing his new design, Grepper said:

> One of the challenges was definitely making sure that every component was of top quality. For example, rather than this being a blender that you can use outside, I wanted it to be a top-quality blender that could make a fantastic margarita, and can produce enough of them to satisfy your event.[6]

One of the benefits of the Kickstarter model was that creators whose projects were shown on this platform could gain a large amount of feedback from funders. They were excited about being able to provide their ideas or ways to improve a product to the designer. One of the objectives of designers was to catch the attention of potential donors by the use of social media (see Boxes 5.1, 5.2 and 5.3 as examples of social media messages from creators).

PROBLEMS

One of the biggest advantages for the designer in seeking Kickstarter funding is that no strings are attached nor is there a loss of control of the project as there would be with equity financing. However, that may be a detractor to someone considering funding a new project. The reason is that many Kickstarter projects run into problems in fulfilling their promises and completing their projects on time. Sometimes the completed projects do not live up to the expectations of funders.

Sometimes supporters of Kickstarter projects may be naïve. The funds they pledge to a project are donations, and rewards are just tokens of thanks. A good example of how that could go wrong is with the iPen, an interactive high-precision stylus for the iPad that was funded on Kickstarter. After some of the funders received their iPens, they were unhappy with its performance and asked for a refund. However, that isn't how Kickstarter works since they did not purchase the pen.

CROWDFUNDING

Definition and Uses

Crowdfunding uses social networks and the interest of individuals to assist people in raising funds. With crowdfunding, it is possible for an individual to help a friend or a community with securing the money needed for a project. Crowdfunding may actually help the diffusion of innovation to occur more rapidly because of the early discussion of the project on the internet (see Box 5.4 entitled "The Diffusion of Innovation.")

One of the greatest benefits of crowdfunding is allowing people to get involved in financing new projects or organizations which had earlier been the sole domain of financial institutions. Some of the advantages of crowdfunding are the following:

1. There is no application process;
2. There are no long wait periods to receive the funds that have been donated;
3. Free crowdfunding sites don't charge a sign-up fee and don't charge a platform fee, allowing one to keep more of what was raised;
4. Crowdfunding takes the fear out of asking for financial help. It is simple to share one's fundraiser with friends and family members on social media; and
5. Crowdfunding makes it easy to reach people outside of one's network.[7]

The reason that people choose crowdfunding to raise money ranges from money for college for a student, medical care and lack of insurance to cover a personal catastrophe. The reason that a great number of crowdfunding projects are to pay for medical expenses is occasioned by the following:

1. Thirty-nine percent of Americans can't afford to spend $400 when faced with an emergency;[8]
2. The retail cost of 267 brand name prescription drugs widely used by older adults has risen in recent years by 5.8 percent;[9]
3. Annual out-of-pocket medical expenses in the United States have risen $486 billion, or an average of $1,242 per person;[10] and
4. Sixty-six percent of people surveyed said that planning for out-of-pocket costs is both the biggest challenge and the most stressful part of health care management.[11]

GoFundMe

The crowdfunding platform GoFundMe asserts that they are the largest social fundraising platform and #1 as the world's most trusted leader in free online fundraising. They allow people to rally support for personal and charitable causes.[12] They also state that their giving community is more than 70 million strong and has raised more than $5 billion.

The steps in obtaining money from this online fundraising site are: Create a fundraiser by telling your story, share that fundraiser via social media and then accept donations that go directly to you or your beneficiary's account. Since the platform is free, an individual can keep more of their money.

Although the company has a Trust and Safety Team that works to prevent misuse of this site, on a few occasions people have made false claims in establishing an account and have received donations. Usually the funds are returned to donors when the misuse is discovered. The GoFundMe organization assists individuals in telling a compelling story and using pictures and videos to help them convince people to give.

A couple of interesting GoFundMe success stories are the following:

1. Walt & Naima's Winter Shelter Wish. Walt was a 7-year-old boy who was concerned about the devastating fire in Northern California. He started a GoFundMe account to benefit a homeless shelter in the area and raised over $11,000.
2. Support Rancho Relaxo's Expansion. A woman named Caitlan started an animal rescue farm to save animals from abuse and neglect. She has raised over $147,000 and saved more than 300 animals.

Indiegogo

This crowdfunding website claims to support a potential fundraiser from the earliest "aha!" moment to the nitty-gritty details of setting up the site. Indiegogo claims the following successes with their platform: $1 billion plus raised across all projects from dance to design, 223 countries and territories are home to Indiegogo users and 18,983 percent is the most a campaign has exceeded its goal, so far. The company also compared their services to those of Kickstarter in Table 5.2.

Table 5.2   Partnerships and support: Indiegogo vs. Kickstarter

Partnerships and Support	Indiegogo	Kickstarter
Design, Prototyping, and Manufacturing Partners		
An innovative program with Arrow will provide all of this	✚	✕
Cutting-Edge Technology		
Support for Apple Pay and integration with Stripe	✚	✕
Fulfillment Partners		
Fulfillment assistance from Amplifier and Brookstone	✚	✕
Retail Partners		
Sell your product on sites including Amazon and Newegg	✚	✕

Source: Indiegogo (n.d.). Evaluating Indiegogo vs. Kickstarter? https://entrepreneur.indiegogo.com/how-it-works/indiegogo-vs-kickstarter/. Accessed September 9, 2019.

EVALUATION OF KICKSTARTER

Kickstarter's stated mission is: "We built Kickstarter to help bring projects to life. We measure our success as a company by how well we achieve that mission, not by the size of our profits." However, more Kickstarter projects have failed to raise the required funds than those that have been successful. In light of that contradiction, the success of Kickstarter would have to be in question.

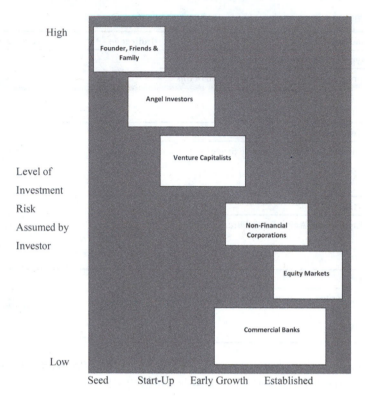

Source: Van Osnabrugge, Mark and Robinson, Robert J. (2000). *Angel Investing.* San Francisco, CA: Jossey-Bass Publishing Company, p. 37.

Figure 5.1   Funding sources for each venture stage

BOX 5.1   GAME DESIGNER'S PLEA TO POTENTIAL FUNDERS

Greetings:

How've you been? I wanted to let you in on a Kickstarter project that your readers simply must know about: KILL UNIT is back!

That's right—the arcade hit from 20 years ago is set for a dramatic revival as the game's creator, Robert Unit, returns to helm KILL UNIT REDUX!

Remarkably, in the 20 years since the original KILL UNIT was a gigantic success, nobody else has made a game about shooting aliens; but with the help of the fans, I aim to change that with KILL UNIT REDUX.

You'll want to mention our sweet Kickstarter rewards. Backers will get exclusive rights to the workings of Robert Unit's "game design mind" as he re-creates the original classic, as well as access to a backers-only forum where fans of the game can talk to each other about how excited they are!

The team is seeking to raise $5,000,000 over the next 10 days. We have a passel of hilarious video diaries (already shot and edited), endorsements from other famous game makers, and Promoted Tweets ready to fire off throughout the fundraising period, so get those reblogging buttons ready! Thanks in advance for your cooperation.

Have a wonderful week,

Sincerely,

MegaSplash PR

Source: Wasteland, M. and Underland, M. (February 1, 2013). Cover my Kickstarter! Kickstarter pleas for media attention. *Game Developer*, 20, No. 2.

BOX 5.2   INDIE GAME DEVELOPER'S PLEA

The Big Dreamer with a Chip on His Shoulder
SUPPORT INDIES!
I am an indie game developer, and I have a Kickstarter and a Greenlight page up for my dream game. It's called My Dream Game. I have written about some of my AMAZING ideas on my Live.Journal, but this has been IGNORED by the big sites.

The game is set on an uninhabited island with a mysterious past. The player must solve ingeniously designed puzzles while proceeding through a complex and non-cliched storyline with over 30 characters and emotional depth. Jaw-dropping graphics and white-knuckled gameplay round out the package. It is somewhat influenced by Final Fantasy, but with other elements as well.

PLEASE SUPPORT INDIES by writing about this project. THE GAME WILL NOT BE MADE unless the word gets out and the project gets more fans. The time is now for gamers to rise up and DEMAND the games they want by backing this project!!!!

The Substitute for Venture Capital

Source: Wasteland, M. and Underland, M. (February 1, 2013). Cover my Kickstarter! Kickstarter pleas for media attention. *Game Developer*, 20, No. 2.

BOX 5.3   PLEA FROM INVENTOR OF SCENTPLAY

Greetings,
Are you content to live in a world where you cannot experience video games with smell? I didn't think so. SensePlay LLC has just launched a Kickstarter for its highly disruptive product, the ScentPlay, and now we need your help to make this revolutionary device a reality.

The heart of the ScentPlay experience is the Scentinjector. This accessory uses high-quality silicone clips to sit comfortably inside the user's nose for hours of olfactory gaming. And, for backers at the $375 level, we will create custom-fitted Scentinjector devices with a custom plastic mold from players' nostrils.

Working prototypes of the ScentPlay system already exist as plans on paper, and some of the industry's top aroma designers are already dreaming up use-case scenarios! We plan on shipping the first units in April.

Thank you,

The SensePlay LLC Team

Source: Wasteland, M. and Underland, M. (February 1, 2013). Cover my Kickstarter! Kickstarter pleas for media attention. *Game Developer*, 20, No. 2.

BOX 5.4   THE DIFFUSION OF INNOVATION

In 1962, E.M. Rogers developed a theory entitled "Diffusion of Innovation". This theory was an attempt to answer the question of how a new product gains momentum and spreads through the economy. The term "adoption" suggests that a person does something differently than what they had done before. This includes purchasing products that they had not purchased in the past. Researchers who have worked with this theory have developed a set of characteristics that they believe define people at each stage of the adoption process. Those stages and personal characteristics are the following (see Figure 5.2):

Innovators – People who are the first to try out a new innovation. These people are adventurous and interested in new ideas. It takes very little promotion to get these people to adopt a new product.

Early Adopters – These people are normally opinion leaders. They like the role of a leader and look forward to the opportunity to change. They need little information to cause them to adopt a new product.

Early Majority – These people are normally not leaders, but they do adopt a product before the average person does. They usually need to actually see the innovation work before they will adopt it. The top of strategies that appeal to this group are success stories from others that the product does what it says it will do.

Late Majority – This group of people are skeptical of change. They will not adopt a product until it has been successfully adopted by the Early Majority. The best strategy to win them over is evidence of how many people have already adopted the product successfully.

Laggards – These are very conservative people and are often bound by tradition. They are extremely skeptical of change and are the hardest consumers to bring on board. The best strategies to bring them aboard would be statistics of products purchased and pressure from people in the other adopter groups.

Organizations selling an innovative product, often try to find the opinion leaders in a particular category in order to get them to buy the product. They know that if they can get opinion leaders to buy, the other potential buyers may eventually be won over.

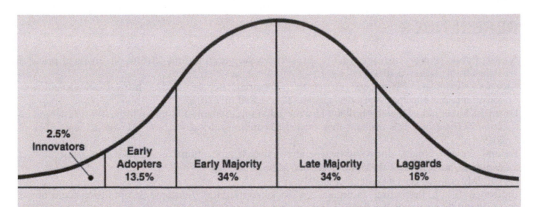

Source: http://blog.leanmonitor.com/early-adopters-allies-launching-product/. Accessed September 2, 2019.

Figure 5.2   Diffusion of innovation model

NOTES

1. Kickstarter website. http://www.kickstarter.com/about/. Accessed September 2, 2019.

2. Ibid.

3. Kickstarter website. http://www.kickstarter.com/press. Accessed May 20, 2020.

4. Ibid.

5. Dormehl, Luke (n.d.). How this brilliant idea earned $11 million on Kickstarter. http://www.fastcompany .com/3034983/how-this-brilliant-idea-earned-$11million-on-kickstarter/. Accessed September 2, 2019.

6. Ibid.

7. GoFundMe.com. Accessed September 2, 2019.

8. Federal Reserve (n.d.). https://www.federalreserve.gov/publications/files/2018-report-economic-well-being -us-households-201905pdf/. Accessed May 20, 2020.

9. AARP Public Policy Institute (n.d.). https://www.aarp.org/ppi/info-2016/trends-in-retail-prices-of-drugs .html. Accessed 2017.

10. Leonhardt, Megan (October 9, 2019). Americans now spend twice as much on health care today as they did in the 1980s. https://www.cnbc.com/2019/10/09/americans-spend-twice-as-much-on-health-care-today-as -in-the-1980s.html. Accessed May 2020.

11. Alegeus Healthcare "Moments of Truth" Research Report (n.d.). https://www.alegeus.com/ consumerismcorner/past-episodes/episode-2. Accessed July 2016.

12. GoFundMe.com. Accessed September 9, 2019.

REFERENCES

AARP Public Policy Institute (n.d.). https://www.aarp.org/ppi/info-2016/trends-in-retail-prices-of -drugs.html. Accessed 2017.

Alegeus Healthcare "Moments of Truth" Research Report (n.d.). https://www.alegeus.com/ consumerismcorner/past-episodes/episode-2. Accessed July 2016.

Dormehl, Luke (n.d.). How this brilliant idea earned $11 million on Kickstarter. http://www.fastcompany .com/3034983/how-this-brilliant-idea-earned-$11million-on-kickstarter/. Accessed September 2, 2019.

Federal Reserve (n.d.). https://www.federalreserve.gov/publications/files/2018-report-economic-well -being-us-households-201905pdf/. Accessed May 20, 2020.

GoFundMe.com. Accessed September 9, 2019.

Indiegogo (n.d.). Evaluating Indiegogo vs. Kickstarter? https://entrepreneur.indiegogo.com/how-it -works/indiegogo-vs-kickstarter/. Accessed September 9, 2019.

Kickstarter website. https://www.kickstarter.com/about/. Accessed May 20, 2020.

Leonhardt, Megan (October 9, 2019). Americans now spend twice as much on health care today as they did in the 1980s. https://www.cnbc.com/2019/10/09/americans-spend-twice-as-much-on-health-care -today-as-in-the-1980s.html. Accessed May 2020.

Van Osnabrugge, Mark and Robinson, Robert J. (2000). *Angel Investing*. San Francisco, CA: Jossey-Bass Publishing Company, p. 37.

Wasteland, M. and Underland, M. (February 1, 2013). Cover my Kickstarter! Kickstarter pleas for media attention. *Game Developer*, 20, No. 2.

6
Securing funding (continued) – Nightlight Donuts: the trials of a collegiate entrepreneur

http://www.nightlightdonuts.com

Jackson Wren threw up in the bank parking lot. He was in the midst of the hardest course in law school; he had a 10-year lease on a property to locate his donut shop that was at a busy intersection in Waco, Texas; his new partner had just quit her job at Magnolia to come full-time with the business; and his guarantor on a half million dollar loan at the bank just announced that he could no longer lend assistance as a backer.

It was March 9, 2020, the first day of Spring Break at Baylor University, and what he had earlier thought would be an exciting time in his life. Jackson had already talked to most of the banks in town, and none of them were interested in lending money to a college kid who had nothing on his balance sheet. At this point, he had to seriously consider whether his dream of a permanent brick-and-mortar location for his Nightlight Donuts would ever be a reality.

THE WREN TWINS

Jackson had an identical twin named Eric. The only way to tell them apart was that one was a bit taller than the other. Even as teenagers, the twins had an entrepreneurial bent. They grew up in Waco where their father was a professor at the Baylor University School of Law. When they were 14, they told their father that they wanted to have a car when they were able to drive. In Texas, one can apply for a driver's license at 16, so they had two years before they could legally drive a car. Their father said he would not pay for a car, so the boys decided to start their own business to earn the money. They came up with an idea for a car detailing business that would be named "Cool Cat Car Care." The twins went from door to door in their neighborhood recruiting customers for their business. They also put flyers in people's mailboxes to increase their coverage. One day the Postmaster of the area called the Wren house, and the twins' mother answered the phone. The Postmaster told Mrs. Wren that her sons had illegally put flyers in mailboxes, and they were now liable for this forbidden activity. She assured the Postmaster that they would never do this again. The boys kept the business for a couple of years until they earned enough money to buy a car.

While the twins were undergraduate students at Baylor University, they started another business called "Dapper Bear." Jackson was an entrepreneurial major, and this was a project in one of his entrepreneurship classes. The company developed a plaid design with the university's colors of green and gold and used the plaid for such items as women's scarves, men's ties, and an assortment of other articles. The business became profitable, so the boys continued to operate it while they were undergraduates.

AN IDEA FOR A NEW BUSINESS

When Jackson and Eric graduated from Baylor, they decided to go to New York to try to break into television by applying to be writers for *Saturday Night Live*. This dream didn't happen, but something else happened while they were in the Big Apple. They lived three floors above a donut shop which was open 24 hours a day, and they watched the large number of people who frequented that establishment. They discovered that the favorite type of donut the shop sold was a croissant donut. The boys decided after a year to return to Waco and open a donut shop in a food truck. The problem was that neither one of them had any experience in cooking. Therefore, before they left New York, they found a man on Craig's List who had made croissant donuts in Paris before coming to New York. Jackson and Eric learned this art from him and purchased his recipe for this delicacy.

When they returned to Waco in 2018, Jackson decided to attend Baylor Law School and get a degree, so Eric had to run the donut food truck they were developing. The twins determined that they needed $60,000 to buy a food truck and have some working capital. They found a company in Portland, Oregon, that constructed the food truck for them. They got their initial capital from friends and family by giving each one a small amount of equity in the company. They knew they would have a difficult time gaining market share in Waco because there was a company that had been around a number of years named Shipley Donuts, and they had gained the majority of the customers in that city of around 130,000 people. This donut shop which had several locations in Waco operated from 5:00 a.m. to 12:00 p.m. Monday through Friday and 1:00 p.m. on the weekend. Therefore, they were not catering to people who wanted donuts at a later hour of the day. However, they did sell kolaches which were filled with fruit or sausage and was a delicacy in the area because of the presence of a Czech community a few miles away.

Launching the Business

The twins launched the business in June of 2018—the same month that Jackson began law school, so Eric had to manage the company initially. At first, they pulled the truck with their mother's 1998 Suburban, but before long it broke down. At that time, Jackson went to a used car company that was going out of business and bought a minivan to pull the truck. He commented that people often thought he was a single dad with this automobile because it was not the typical car driven by a college guy.

Jackson recalled that his stress level was already high in June of 2018 because that month he started law school, launched a business, started dating a new girl friend and bought a dog. His schedule at that time was to arise at 4:00 a.m. to study, attend law school from 7:45 a.m. to 3:30 p.m., go home and study until 10:00 or 11:00 p.m.

The donut food truck did better the first year than they had anticipated (see Table 6.2 entitled "Nightlight Donuts 2018 and 2019, profit and loss statements"). After that year, Eric decided to go to graduate school at Northwestern University, so Jackson bought him out by paying for his tuition. Now that Jackson was the primary twin running the business, he had to get up at 2:30 a.m. to prepare the donuts before going to law school. He hired a girl for $30,000 a year to help with the business, but she left after seven months because the job was so isolated. Jackson did not have an office, and the kitchen in the food truck was not large enough; so he had to do all of the preparation of the donuts in the commissary he was using. The City of Waco required that all food trucks had to be associated with a commissary for the preparation of the food. His commissary was in a non-profit business called "Jesus Said Love," and he paid $1,000 a month for that location. He got the maximum number of location permits he could get from the City which was two in order to park in front of a coffee shop and a bar at various times of the day and night. Jackson also found suppliers of his ingredients that gave him a good price, and he had an agreement with them to continue to supply his store after he left the food truck.

In March of 2020, he recruited a young lady to help him named Kate. She had run track for the University of Michigan, and this business was her dream job. She had been working at Magnolia which was the home base for the television show named the *Fixer Upper* hosted by Joanna and Chip Gaines. That same month, Jackson began looking for a location for a brick-and-mortar donut shop. He looked for some land near Baylor University big enough to have room for a drive-through at the shop; but because there was a major highway construction operation going on in that area, he decided to look elsewhere. Locating in downtown Waco was out of the question because there was insufficient space for a drive-through which he believed was an essential for the business.

It was about this time that the COVID-19 virus occurred, and he would discover later that having a drive-through operation was a very good idea because restaurants had to close down inside seating for several months. It was Jackson's contention that because customers had shifted their purchasing habits for food to drive-throughs during the pandemic, that they would continue to make use of such facilities in the future. Because of the COVID-19 virus, the City of Waco closed down all food trucks in town. Jackson wondered what he could do to keep his employees working. He arrived at an idea that would both keep his employees attached to the business and supply a needed device to local hospitals. He bought eight sewing machines at a discount and employed his workers making masks. The N-95 masks (the type required by health care facilities) were then donated to hospitals who had a shortage of these devices. By the end of this project, his employees had made about 5,000 masks.

Securing the Funding

What Jackson needed the most was someone with capital to invest in his business. He met a man named Roy who seemed to be that person. Roy had a business that furnished such things as trash cans, roll-off bins, and so on to trash collection services. Jackson was 28 years old at the time; and when bankers looked at him, they immediately decided that he was too young to take on an operation such as he was proposing. Roy said he was interested in investing in his startup, so Jackson was relieved that this big decision was out of the way.

There was a property available at the corner of two very busy highways in Waco with enough room for a double-lane drive-through, and Jackson agreed with the landlord for a 10-year lease (see Figure 6.1 entitled "Possible location for Nightlight Donuts"). The landlord was in the process of developing the property and was delighted to secure Jackson's interest. However, Jackson needed a guarantor who would stand behind the 10-year lease and behind a note at a bank that would be about $500,000 and a 20 percent down payment on the loan. It appeared that Roy was the person who could get the financing for all of this. Jackson was delighted and relieved. The arrangement the two agreed upon was that Roy would have a 30 percent equity position in the business, and Jackson would have a 70 percent position.

The first day of Spring Break (Monday, March 9), Roy called Jackson and said he needed to meet him immediately at the bank where he had secured an option on the loan. Kate also called that day and told Jackson that she had quit her job at Magnolia and was now ready to begin her job with him the next day. When Roy arrived, he said that the bank had decided not to go through with the loan because of the pandemic, so he could no longer help Jackson with the business. Now Jackson needed $500,000 from a bank and a guarantor on the 10-year lease for the location. He had already spent $25,000 with an architect for a design for the building. When Jackson told the landlord that his guarantor had backed out, the landlord was furious because he said he had already committed $100,000 to the project himself. He also told Jackson that if he did not go through with the lease, he would sue him.

Research for the Venture

In 2019, Jackson sat outside a number of donut shops in Waco and watched the people coming and going from those establishments. He made note of the times when traffic was the heaviest and what items the people purchased. He noticed that many people bought donuts later in the day. He had found with the food truck that between 7:30 and 11:30 p.m. donuts would fly off the shelves. During that four-hour period of time, he would sell out in 1½ hours with around 900 to 1,200 donuts.

Operations of the Shop

Jackson intended to hire about 35–45 employees. Of that number, he planned to have about one-third full-time and two-thirds part-time employees. He decided to pay his employees a $14 per hour starting salary as an incentive to get the best employees that he could find. When

Jackson posted an ad for employees, he got 400 applicants the first week. He narrowed the applicants down to 150 and intended to interview every one of these applicants in one week.

The hours of the business would be the following:

3:00 to 5:00 a.m. – Donut prep

5:00 to 7:00 a.m. – Drive-through open

7:00 a.m. to 10:00 p.m. – Inside dining

Weekends open until midnight

Jackson planned to partner with Intelligentsia Coffee in Chicago for his coffee. He became familiar with this coffee when he was in New York and subsequently contacted them about furnishing the coffee for his shop. Jackson decided to keep the menu simple. He intended to offer only six types of donuts plus donut holes. The luncheon menu would consist of one donut sandwich which would be glazed and filled with a stuffing.

INDUSTRY BACKGROUND

IBISWorld's industry data on "Doughnut Stores" indicates that this industry has been very profitable from 2014 to 2019. For example, the industry had an annual growth rate of 11.5 percent, an average profit margin of 7.7 percent and an annual growth rate of 3.4 percent during that five-year period.[1] Over the five years leading to 2024, industry revenue was projected to increase at an annualized rate of 1.1 percent to $8.7 billion. Product innovation and an added variety of products were expected to be the primary means of increasing revenue.

In terms of products and services segmentation, donuts by the dozen accounted for an average of 48.4 percent, individual donuts accounted for 39.6 percent and beverages and other products accounted for 12.0 percent of the sales in 2018. The revenue volatility was low in this industry and capital intensity was medium. There was light regulation in the industry and low industry globalization. Barriers into the industry were low, but competition was high and increasing.

The drivers of consumption in the industry were consumer spending, per capita coffee consumption, the consumer confidence index and an increase in consumers' desire for healthy eating. There has also been an increase in gluten-free donuts for consumers with dietary restrictions. In addition, donut stores have relied more and more on coffee sales to generate sales for donuts.

The industry has been more labor- than capital-intensive. Most donut shops have relied on a high level of customer service to generate sales. The industry uses less cooking equipment than most fast food restaurants because franchises tend to outsource products to maintain quality and reduce costs. Table 6.1 shows the major market segmentation of donut shops based upon the time of day donuts are purchased.

The West Region of the United States had the largest concentration of donut shops with 24.4 percent of the total. California had about 15.0 percent of the nation's donut stores. Other states that had a high concentration of donut stores were New York (7.5 percent), Texas (5.6 percent), Florida (4.8 percent) and Washington (4.8 percent).

Table 6.1   Major market segmentation

Time of day	Percentage of donuts purchased
Mid-morning customers (8 a.m. to 11 a.m.)	30.0%
Lunchtime customers (11 a.m. to 3 p.m.)	22.2%
Nighttime customers (10 p.m. to 4 a.m.)	14.3%
Dinnertime customers (6 p.m. to 10 p.m.)	13.0%
Early morning customers (4 a.m. to 8 a.m.)	12.4%
Afternoon customers (3 p.m. to 6 p.m.)	8.1%

Source: Kumar, Tanvi (May 2019). *IBISWorld.* US Specialized Industry Report on Doughnut Stores.

THE COVID-19 PANDEMIC

The coronavirus (also known as COVID-19) was first identified by the World Health Organization (WHO) in December of 2019 in Wuhan, China. Then in March of 2020, the WHO declared that the virus was a pandemic. The illness was believed to have been spread by small droplets produced by coughing, sneezing and talking by people in close proximity to one another.[2] Another theory suggested that people could become infected by touching a contaminated surface and then touching their face.

Symptoms of the virus were fever, cough, shortness of breath, tiredness and loss of the sense of smell or taste. The approximate time between a person's exposure to the virus and their showing symptoms of the illness ranged from two to fourteen days.[3] Some of the complications of the virus were pneumonia and acute respiratory distress syndrome.

The recommended precautions people were warned to take to prevent the spread of the disease were handwashing, the wearing of a mask and keeping at least a six-foot distance from other people. Global authorities suggested the closing of schools and non-essential businesses and a limitation on travel within and between countries.

The economic impact of COVID-19 was devastating to most economies of the world. With the closing of businesses, unemployment became widespread. Governments made decisions about the deployment of resources to help businesses and individuals survive the pandemic. At the beginning of Spring Break for most schools in the United States in March of 2020, there was a great deal of uncertainty about the future of local, national and world economies and the death toll that would result from the virus.

DECISION TIME

Jackson reflected on what was happening to him and wondered if there was still a way that he could make his plan work and open his business. He knew his idea for a donut shop that would be open in the evening as well as the morning was a good idea. The food truck had proved that. However, because of his inexperience and age, he had not been able to get a single bank in town to loan him the money to secure the location and fixtures he would need. What could he do next? Were there any other stones that he had not yet turned over?

Table 6.2   Nightlight Donuts 2018 and 2019, profit and loss statements

	2018	2019
Income	36,718.74	142,219.95
Cost of goods sold	11,513.07	33,418.78
Gross profit	25,205.67	108,801.17
Expenses		
Bank charges and fees	42.25	301.67
Car and truck	2,714.46	1,348.53
Charitable contributions	00.00	575.00
Computer expenses	00.00	277.16
Contractors	3,688.84	320.00
Depreciation expense	7,731.00	00.00
Dues & subscriptions	246.33	835.18
Gifts	221.55	00.00
Guaranteed payments	12,800.00	00.00
Insurance	1,934.67	1,793.22
Interest paid	258.99	2,292.35
Job supplies	4,878.53	4,749.67
Legal and professional services	400.00	00.00
Licenses and permits	300.00	480.00
Meals and entertainment	255.93	1,393.41
Miscellaneous	456.70	311.03
Total payroll expenses	8,050.10	70,589.71
Rent and lease	4,861.50	9,065.00
Repairs and maintenance	990.74	909.58
Sponsorships	2,713.30	00.00
Taxes	772.82	00.00
Training	8.00	00.00
Utilities	28.87	00.00
Total expenses	**53,354.58**	**95,241.51**
Net operating income	(28,148.91)	13,559.66
Total other income	00.00	123.72
Net income	(28,148.91)	13,683.38

Figure 6.1 Possible location for Nightlight Donuts

NOTES

1. Kumar, Tanvi (May 2019). *IBISWorld*. US Specialized Industry Report on Doughnut Stores.
2. UN News (July 1, 2020). Stalled Security Council resolution adopted, backing UN's global humanitarian ceasefire call. https://news.un.org/en/story/2020/07/1067552. Accessed August 12, 2020.
3. UN News (June 24, 2020). COVID-19: Recovery will be slower following "crisis like no other," IMF predicts. https://news.un.org/en/story/2020/06/1067052. Accessed August 12, 2020.

REFERENCES

Kumar, Tanvi (May 2019). *IBISWorld*. US Specialized Industry Report on Doughnut Stores.
UN News (June 24, 2020). COVID-19: Recovery will be slower following "crisis like no other," IMF predicts. https://news.un.org/en/story/2020/06/1067052. Accessed August 12, 2020.
UN News (July 1, 2020). Stalled Security Council resolution adopted, backing UN's global humanitarian ceasefire call. https://news.un.org/en/story/2020/07/1067552. Accessed August 12, 2020.

7
Developing a new business model – Etsy: will the desire for economic success overwhelm creativity?

http://www.etsy.com

On April 16, 2015, Etsy issued an initial public offering (IPO) at $16 a share. In the first days of trading, the company's share price nearly doubled to $31. However, in 2016 the company entered a period of continued decline until the price of a share of their stock came in at $6.90 on February 8, 2016.[1] Although the stock had worked its way back up to $57 per share as of October 22, 2019, there were those who feared for the future of the company. The concern of artisans who sold their products on the site was that the drive for greater financial success as evidenced by the IPO could indicate that the emphasis on smaller craft companies might be abandoned in a search for larger, more profitable operations. As evidence of this, in the period from 2015 to 2018, the revenues of Etsy grew at a faster pace than that of its sellers (see Table 7.1 entitled "Gross merchandise sales (GMS) by Etsy sellers and revenue by Etsy from 2015 to 2019"; Table 7.3 entitled "Etsy consolidated statements of operations 2016–2018"; and Table 7.4 entitled "Etsy's consolidated balance sheets 2017–2019"). By 2020, there was a concern that smaller craft artists might seek a website of their own with less clutter and that shareholders might leave because of the B Corporation status of the company.

BACKGROUND ON ETSY

In June of 2005, Etsy was founded as an online marketplace for handmade goods. The founders of the company located in Brooklyn, New York, were Robert Kalin, Chris Maguire and Haim Schoppik.

Etsy was established as a peer-to-peer (P2P) e-commerce website that allowed sellers and buyers to interact in the offering of handmade crafts, vintage items, art and photography. The marketplace worked very much like Amazon and eBay; however, Etsy relied more on unique items rather than those that were mass produced.

A company's business model is the way they intend to generate revenue. The development of the model should allow the organizers to understand, develop and utilize an effective method for creating and delivering value to its customers. Etsy's business model consisted of acquiring revenues from the following sources:

1. Listing fee paid by Etsy craft artists ($0.20) for each item listed;
2. Fees paid by Etsy craft artists for each completed transaction (a 3.5 percent fee for sales completed on the website);
3. Fees for seller services which included services such as prominent placement in search results via Promoted Listings;
4. Payment processing via Direct Checkout;
5. Purchasing of shipping labels through Etsy's platform; and
6. Fees received from a third-party payment processor.

The average sale on Etsy was between $15 and $20. Most of the sellers on the site were women who were college educated and in their 20s and 30s.[2]

Robert Kalin, one of the founders, suggested that he named the site Etsy because he wanted a no-nonsense word since they were building their brand from scratch. He had been watching Fellini's movie entitled "8½" and writing down what he was hearing. He noticed that in the Italian language people often say "etsi" (which means "oh, yes"), and he believed he had found a unique name for the company.[3]

Chad Dickerson joined Etsy in 2008 as its first Chief Technology Officer. Then in 2011 he became the company's CEO and began championing the "re-imagining of commerce." The company continued to add more tools and functionality to gain greater exposure for its sellers' products. That year, the company introduced a Facebook-like social networking system called People Search so that buyers and sellers could connect with one another and become friends.[4]

Under Dickerson's leadership, Etsy grew quickly and became a certified B Corporation in 2012. This seal for ethical corporations was awarded by the non-profit B Lab. It was a new corporate form designed to protect firms that had a distinct social mission from shareholders who would demand an early profit. In fact, Etsy did go public before making a profit.

In order to receive this award, a company is required to meet standards related to the environment, workers and suppliers. There are presently about 2,000 companies that are B Corps including Patagonia, Warby Parker and Kickstarter, and most of these companies are privately held. Only Etsy and one other company are traded on a major United States stock exchange.[5] The reason so few companies that have B Corp status are publicly traded is the fear by most companies that stockholders might believe that having the designation will put other goals above that of profit maximization. However, Dickerson believed that big institutional investors, who were its primary shareholders, could be convinced that Etsy's community focus and B Corp status were not incompatible with growth and profitability.[6]

From its beginning, Etsy had many fans who applauded the online marketplace as "an antidote to global mass production and consumption and a stand against corporate branding."[7] By 2016, Etsy had become the fifth most visited marketplace site in the United States surpassed only by Amazon, eBay, Walmart and Best Buy.

Mission

In 2018, Etsy introduced a new set of guiding principles which served as their North Star and reflected how the company desired to act. These guiding principles were the following:

- **We commit to our craft**. Our work has the power to change lives. That's why we strive to learn continuously and excel at what we do.
- **We minimize waste**. Time, resources, and energy are precious, so we focus only on what will have the greatest impact.
- **We embrace differences**. Diverse teams are stronger, and inclusive cultures are more resilient. When we seek out different perspectives, we make better decisions and build better products.
- **We dig deeper**. The best solutions to meaningful challenges are rarely easy or obvious. We stay curious, balance our intuition with insights, and decide with confidence.
- **We lead with optimism**. We believe in our mission, and we believe in each other. We see the world as it is, set ambitious goals, and inspire one another with generosity of spirit. Together, we reimagine what is possible.[8]

Outcomes

As of December 31, 2019, the Etsy and Reverb (used instrument marketplace Etsy bought in August 2019) sites connected 2.7 million active sellers to 46.4 million active buyers. Their buyers and sellers were located worldwide with the six main markets being in the United States, Australia, France, Germany, the United Kingdom and Canada. By 2019, the company had connected more buyers and sellers than ever before and delivered a strong performance across important financial and operating matrices. This is evidenced by Table 7.1 entitled "Gross merchandise sales by Etsy sellers and revenue by Etsy from 2015 to 2019."

Table 7.1 Gross merchandise sales (GMS) by Etsy sellers and revenue by Etsy from 2015 to 2019

	2015	2016	2017	2018	2019 (not including Reverb)
Gross Merchandise Sales	$2.39B	$2.84B	$3.25B	$3.93B	$4.7B
Etsy Revenue	$273M	$365M	$441M	$604M	$799M

Source: Etsy (2019). Annual report for 2019. https://investors.etsy.com/financials/annual-reports-and-proxy/default.aspx. Accessed September 15, 2019.

Three Bird Nest

Although 65 percent of Etsy's sellers made less than $100 a year on their shops, there was one seller who made almost $1 million a year. Her name was Alicia Shaffer, and her business was called Three Bird Nest. This unusual name was derived from a bird's nest tattoo Shaffer had which honored her three children. This entrepreneur lived in Livermore, California, and sold her assortment of 58 designs including socks, leg warmers, scarves and lace headbands on Etsy's website. The prices of her goods ranged from $4 for a fabric cuff bracelet to $38 for a floral scarf. Due to the success of her business, by early 2016, Shaffer was employing 15 sewers, a photographer to shoot pictures of items for advertisements and was even sourcing some items from India.[9]

According to the 2020 seller survey:

83 percent identify as women

66 percent consider their Etsy shop to be a business

95 percent run their shops from their homes

82 percent aspire to grow their sales in the future

64 percent started their Etsy shop as a way to supplement income.

The 2020 seller survey found that 29 percent of Etsy sellers were pursuing their creative business as their sole occupation.

In keeping with Etsy's B Corp status, the company had committed to using their power as a business to have an impact on the world in the following ways:

1. Economic impact
   Make creating entrepreneurship a path to economic security and personal empowerment. Double U.S. Etsy sellers' economic output by 2023.
   Invest in social programs that foster economic security and personal empowerment by our stakeholders.
   Advance public policies that increase economic security and reduce administrative burdens for creative entrepreneurs.
2. Social impact
   Enable equitable access to the opportunities that we create.
   Approximately double the percentage of Etsy's workforce by 2023.
   Build a diverse, equitable and sustainable supply chain to support our operations and bring value to both Etsy and our vendors.
   Make Etsy a more inclusive and welcoming marketplace for people from underrepresented backgrounds.
3. Ecological impact
   Build long-term resilience by eliminating our carbon impacts and fostering responsible resource use.
   Utilize and source energy responsibly so that we can power our operations with 100 percent renewable electricity by 2020 and reduce the intensity of our energy use by 25 percent by 2025.
   Become the first major online shopping destination to offset 100 percent of emissions from shipping, completing the journey to become a carbon-neutral company.
   Complete certification of all of Etsy's core offices to become TRUE Zero Waste Facilities through the U.S. Green Building Council's certification program.[10]

The company had a generous parental leave policy that allowed both parents six months off. They also offered free craft classes and a very elaborate meal plan for employees. Meals were offered twice weekly catered by socially conscious and high-end restaurants. The leftover food was composted locally as a part of Etsy's plan to send almost no waste to landfills by 2020. In the beginning of this program, food scraps were packed onto a Dutch cargo bike, and an "office ecologist" would pedal several miles to a Brooklyn farm for disposal.[11]

COMPETITORS

The two largest online marketplaces in the United States were Amazon.com and eBay.com. The original goal of Amazon was to replicate a catalog business online. However, eBay had a different strategy. This company recognized the great potential in uniting buyers and sellers in an online auction.

Amazon was launched in Seattle, Washington, as an online bookseller, but the company grew into the likeness of such big retailers as Walmart and Target. The products they sold ranged from cookware to hardware and everything in between. The rapid growth of Amazon occurred at the expense of profitability.

eBay had a much slower growth than Amazon. The focus of the company was always on hosting an auction site where buyers and sellers would meet and enter into mutually beneficial transactions.

The Initial Public Offerings (IPOs) of the two companies were strikingly parallel. Both initially offered shares of stocks at a price of $18. However, at the end of the first day of trading, Amazon's stock price was $30 and eBay stock ended at $47.37.

Since their IPOs, the stock prices went in opposite directions. The rise and fall of Amazon's share price since its IPO illustrated the rise and fall of the dot-com companies. Its stock price rose from $18 to over $100 in 2000 and then fell to the original price again. On the other hand, eBay's stock price showed a steady consistency in profitability.[12] In 2014, Amazon's sales amounted to $88.99 billion while eBay's total sales were $17.94 billion.

By 2019, Amazon's sales were $280.5 billion and eBay's sales were $10.8 billion.[13]

On May 28, 2020, eBay's stock was at $44.23 on Nasdaq while Amazon's stock was at $2,401 on Nasdaq and Etsy's stock was priced at $77.90.[14]

These two companies were the biggest competitors in the online marketplace industry; however, Etsy, Inc. had a distinctly different initial strategy. That unique strategy was to offer a site for craft artists to sell their handmade products.

Smaller competitors that would be considered direct competitors to Etsy are shown in Table 7.2.

Table 7.2 Etsy's direct competitors

Company Name	Country	Focus
Artfire	Tucson, Arizona, U.S.	Handmade, vintage
Amazon Handmade	United States	Custom artisan
Bonanza.com	United States	Clothing and fashion
Zibbet	Australia	Online craft marketplace
Hello Pretty	South Africa	Online craft marketplace
Tindie	Oregon, United States	Technology and electronics

Source: Best Etsy alternatives (n.d.). https://onextrapixel.com/best-etsy-alternatives/. Accessed August 5, 2019.

CHALLENGES FOR ETSY

Some of the challenges for Etsy in 2019 and beyond were the following:

1. In October of 2013, Etsy had introduced new guidelines that allowed their sellers to hire employees. In the past, a seller had to be an independent operator. Some sellers feared that this would cause sellers to become much larger and lose the original craft feel of the website.
2. The October 2013 guidelines also allowed sellers to use manufacturers to produce their designs rather than maintaining their exclusive handmade design platform.
3. In May of 2017, one of the company's largest investors, Seth Wunder, accused Dickerson and the Etsy board of overspending and of failing to take investors' concerns seriously. Shortly after that, Etsy announced that 80 employees had been laid off, and Dickerson had been fired. Dickerson was replaced by Josh Silverman who was a former American Express executive who had also worked for eBay.
4. In one quarter of 2017, over 30,000 sellers were flagged by Etsy for investigation because of suspicious behavior, and some of the shops were closed. The flagged shops were suspected of violating the company's rules.
5. An individual's branding was often lost in a sea of sellers which might not occur if the seller had a separate website.
6. Sellers were at the mercy of getting a bad review by buyers that might severely restrict their sales.

THE FUTURE

Initially, Wall Street analysts were delighted with Etsy's public offering. However, several years later some of the sellers on the website had concerns that the smaller sellers would become less important to the company. Cherri Rodriguez had been selling hand crocheted Rasta hats on Etsy for a decade. However, by 2019 she was worried that now that Etsy was a public company, the investors' appetite for growth would make doing business there difficult for small sellers.[15] In addition, there was a further concern by some of the investors that Etsy's classification as a B Corp might cause the company to place less emphasis on profits and more on environmental issues.

INCOME STATEMENTS OF ETSY

Table 7.3 Etsy's consolidated statements of operations 2016–2018 (in thousands except share and per share amounts)

	2019	2018	2017
Revenue	$818,379	$603,693	$441,231
Cost of revenue	$271,036	$190,762	$150,986
Gross profit	$547,343	$412,931	$290,245
Operating expenses			
Marketing	$215,570	$158,013	$109,085
Product development	$121,878	$97,249	$74,616
General and administrative	$121,134	$82,883	$91,486
Asset impairment charges			$3,162
Total operating expenses	$458,582	$338,145	$278,349
Income from operations	$88,761	$74,786	$11,896
Other (expense) income:			
Interest expense	$(24,320)	$(22,178)	$11,130
Interest and other income	$13,199	$8,957	$2,394
Foreign exchange (loss) gain	$3,006	$(6,487)	$29,105
Total other (expense) income	$(8,115)	$(19,708)	$20,369
Income (loss) before income taxes	$80,646	$55,078	$32,265
Benefit (provision) for income taxes	$15,248	$22,413	$49,535
Net income (loss)	$95,894	$77,491	$81,800
Net income (loss) per share attributable to common stockholders:			
Basic	$0.80	$0.64	$0.69
Diluted	$0.76	$0.61	$0.68

Table 7.4 Etsy consolidated balance sheets 2017–2019 (in thousands except share and per share amounts)

	2019	2018	2017
ASSETS			
Current assets:			
Cash and cash equivalents	$443,293	$366,985	$315,442
Short-term investments	$373,959	$257,302	$25,108
Accounts receivable, net	$15,386	$12,244	$33,667
Prepaid and other assets	$38,614	$22,686	$20,379
Funds receivable and other accounts	$48,786	$21,072	$44,658
Total current assets	$920,038	$680,289	$439,254
Restricted cash	$5,341	$5,341	$5,341
Property and equipment, net	$144,864	$120,179	$117,617
Goodwill	$138,731	$37,482	$38,541
Intangible assets, net	$199,236	$34,589	$4,100
Deferred tax assets	$14,257	$23,464	$159
Other assets	$29,542	$507	$561
Total assets	$1,452,009	$901,851	$605,573
LIABILITIES AND STOCKHOLDERS' EQUITY			
Current liabilities:			
Accounts payable	$26,324	$26,545	$13,622
Accrued expenses	$88,345	$49,158	$28,743
Capital lease obligations – current	$8,274	$3,884	$5,798
Funds payable and amounts due to sellers	$49,786	$21,072	$44,658
Deferred revenue	$7,617	$7,478	$6,262
Other current liabilities	$8,181	$3,925	$3,394
Total current liabilities	$188,527	$112,062	$102,477
Finance lease obligations – net of current portion	53,611	2,095	4,115
Deferred tax liabilities	64,497	30,455	23,786
Facility financing obligation	-	59,991	60,049
Long-term debt, net	785,126	276,486	-
Other liabilities	43,956	19,864	18,262
Total liabilities	1,135,718	500,953	208,689
Total stockholders' equity	406,634	400,898	396,894
Total liabs. & stockholders' equity	$1,542,352	$901,851	$605,583

Source: Etsy (2019). Annual report for 2019. https://investors.etsy.com/financials/annual-reports-and-proxy/default.aspx. Accessed September 15, 2019.

NOTES

1. Depersio, Greg (November 8, 2018; updated October 22, 2019). Etsy: How it's fared since its IPO. *Investopedia.* https://www.investopedia.com/articles/markets/012716/etsy-how-its-fared-its-2015-ipo-etsy.asp. Accessed September 16, 2019.

2. Miller, Kerry (June 12, 2007). Etsy: A site for artisans takes off. *Business Week.*

3. Lammie, Rob (2011). How Etsy, eBay, Reddit got their names. *Mental Floss*, CNN.

4. Tabuchi, Hiroko (March 15, 2015). Etsy's success gives rise to problems of credibility and scale. *The New York Times.*

5. Chafkin, Max and Cao, Jing (May 22, 2017). Leave my Etsy alone. *Bloomberg Businessweek*, Issue 4523. Accessed September 16, 2019.

6. Ibid.

7. Tabuchi, Hiroko (March 15, 2015). Etsy's success gives rise to problems of credibility and scale. *The New York Times.*

8. Etsy (2018). Annual report for 2018. https://investors.etsy.com/financials/annual-reports-and-proxy/default .aspx. Accessed August 7, 2019.

9. How one woman makes almost $1 million a year on Etsy (February 12, 2015). *Fast Company*. https://www .fastcompany.com/3042352/how-one-knitter-makes-almost-1-million-a-year-on-etsy?cid-search. Accessed June 15, 2019.

10. Etsy's annual report for 2018.

11. Chafkin, Max and Cao, Jing (May 22, 2017). Leave my Etsy alone. *Bloomberg Businessweek*, Issue 4523. Accessed September 16, 2019.

12. Krishnamurthy, Sandeep (2004). A comparative analysis of eBay and Amazon. *Idea Group, Inc.* https://www .researchgate.net/publication/314480267/. Accessed March 3, 2021.

13. https://www.macrotrends.net. Accessed July 7, 2019.

14. https://www.marketwatch.com/investing/stock/amzn. Accessed August 17, 2019.

15. Picker, Leslie (February 16, 2015). Will Etsy come undone by success? *Bloomberg Businessweek*, Issue 4415, pp. 22–23.

REFERENCES

Best Etsy alternatives (n.d.). https://onextrapixel.com/best-etsy-alternatives/. Accessed August 5, 2019.

Chafkin, Max and Cao, Jing (May 22, 2017). Leave my Etsy alone. *Bloomberg Businessweek*, Issue 4523. Accessed September 16, 2019.

Depersio, Greg (November 8, 2018; updated October 22, 2019). Etsy: How it's fared since its IPO. *Investopedia.* https://www.investopedia.com/articles/markets/012716/etsy-how-its-fared-its-2015 -ipo-etsy.asp. Accessed September 16, 2019.

Etsy (2018). Annual report for 2018. https://investors.etsy.com/financials/annual-reports-and-proxy/ default.aspx. Accessed August 7, 2019.

Etsy (2019). Annual report for 2019. https://investors.etsy.com/financials/annual-reports-and-proxy/ default.aspx. Accessed September 15, 2019.

How one woman makes almost $1 million a year on Etsy (February 12, 2015). *Fast Company*. http://www .fastcodesign.com/3042352/.net/stocks/charts/. Accessed June 15, 2019.

https://www.macrotrends.net. Accessed July 7, 2019.

https://www.marketwatch.com/investing/stock/amzn. Accessed August 17, 2019.

Krishnamurthy, Sandeep (2004). A comparative analysis of eBay and Amazon. *Idea Group, Inc.* https:// www.researchgate.net/publication/314480267/. Accessed March 3, 2021.

Lammie, Rob (2011). How Etsy, eBay, Reddit got their names. *Mental Floss*, CNN.

Miller, Kerry (June 12, 2007). Etsy: A site for artisans takes off. *Business Week.*

Picker, Leslie (February 16, 2015). Will Etsy come undone by success? *Bloomberg Businessweek*, Issue 4415, pp. 22–23.

Tabuchi, Hiroko (March 15, 2015). Etsy's success gives rise to problems of credibility and scale. *The New York Times.*

8

Assessing the role of the entrepreneur – Revival Restaurant: revitalizing a dormant neighborhood

http://www.revivaleastsideeatery.com

Danielle Young, a co-owner of Revival Restaurant, live streamed Governor Abbott's press conference and awaited the notice that non-essential businesses would have to close due to the coronavirus pandemic. The primary exception was for restaurants that served curbside. She and her husband had opened the restaurant on July 19, 2019 and only recently had the traffic through the front door really begun to pick up. Danielle, like many other business owners around the country, had to decide whether to close her restaurant or find some alternative way to remain open, be profitable and retain employees on the payroll.

BACKGROUND ON THE YOUNGS

Danielle Young grew up in Asheville, North Carolina, and graduated from the University of North Carolina at Chapel Hill with a psychology degree. Travis was raised in San Antonio, Texas, and received his degree in marketing from Texas A&M University at Corpus Christi. After graduation, Danielle went to work for a church and Travis accepted a position with Young Life as a counselor.[1] During the summer of 2008, both Danielle and Travis decided to go on a mission trip with Young Life to Uganda. It was there that the two met and fell in love. The next year they were married and Danielle moved to Corpus Christi, Texas, where they remained for two years. In 2011, the couple moved to Waco, Texas, so that Danielle could earn her doctorate in psychology from Baylor University. Travis immediately was hired with a marketing company named Hole in the Roof. The couple made many friends who shared their interests and tastes in food in their new hometown.

BECOMING AN ENTREPRENEUR

Although Danielle had always liked to cook, she would never have guessed that cooking would become her primary activity. The idea for the restaurant began one summer day in 2017 when she and Travis were driving around Waco looking for a local place to eat dinner. She wanted a place where she could get a delicious salad that didn't have iceberg lettuce and Travis could get a healthy hamburger. Unfortunately, they never did find such a restaurant in town, so they started a conversation about the possibility of starting their own farm-to-market restaurant using products from the Waco area.

Business Plan

No one had ever accused Danielle of being a risk taker. Although she had heard people suggest in the past that entrepreneurs could always be identified as risk takers, she knew she didn't fit into that category. She avoided risks at all costs and was extremely conservative in controlling her spending. An example of that was that she had kept her last car for 17 years. She worked hard at putting together a business plan that would reflect her affinity for controlling costs.

Danielle initially stated, "How difficult could it be to start a restaurant?" As she progressed in developing her business plan, she discovered that restaurants had the highest mortality rate of any type of business. She meticulously identified the cost of every item that she would use in the business and how long each component would last. She worked timelessly on coming up with a list of monthly expenses even to the smallest detail such as the kilowatt hours per month the restaurant would use and how often the grease trap would have to be emptied.

When her plan was finished, she went to a local bank to apply for a small business loan. Unfortunately, the banker refused her application because she was a woman. He said to her, "If I were your Dad, I would tell you not to open a restaurant." He also warned her, "If you do open a restaurant, your marriage will probably end in a divorce." Another bank, however, did give her the loan, and that bank continued to be a good friend to her in the development of her business. Danielle and Travis were also able to get some TIF (Tax Increment Fund) money in the amount of $111,000 for the exterior façade of the restaurant.

Location

The City of Waco originated on the east side of the Brazos River that runs through the middle of the town. The main street in that area was Elm Avenue; and at one time, it was a bustling main street in that area of town. However, some severe rains caused flooding of the Brazos River, and Elm Avenue was flooded so frequently that most businesses fled to higher ground on the west side of the river. For many years, Elm Avenue fell into disrepair until a man named Doug Brown began to buy up every parcel of land he could find along Elm and the contiguous area. In the early 2000s, Brown began encouraging people to come back to Elm and help it thrive again. Unfortunately, Brown died unexpectedly just as he was beginning to sell his idea of revitalizing his area. One of the people who bought some of his parcels of land was Dr. Nancy Grayson who started a coffee shop/bakery named Lula Jane after her grandmother.

Danielle and Travis visited Lula Jane's often and began to receive encouragement from Nancy to buy part of a parcel of land she had in the 700 block of Elm. The building had been a church named Waco Community Baptist Church. Nancy planned to open up part of the building as a non-profit grocery store, and she suggested that Danielle and Travis could locate their restaurant next door. This seemed reasonable to Danielle and Travis, so they bought the parcel and began the renovation of the former church. (See Figure 8.1 entitled "Exterior of Revival Restaurant.") In the meantime, other parcels of land were being purchased from Doug Brown's children, Sam and Cathy, and plans were being made to build apartments, retail space, a boot store and an ice cream parlor at the beginning of Elm next to the Brazos (which by now had been protected from flooding).

Gentrification[2]

The residents in the Elm Avenue neighborhood were delighted with the plans to revitalize the area, but they often voiced a concern about the increased value of their property under the revitalization process. The idea of gentrification worried them because as more people bought and revitalized space in the area, the value of the property would go up and so would their taxes which had stayed the same for a long period of time. Some people suggested that these residents should be grandfathered in on the tax registrar with a clause that would keep their property taxes the same for ten years so that they could continue to afford to live in the area. Many of them had their houses passed down to them by their parents or grandparents and could not pay higher taxes.

Employees

Before she began, Danielle hired a chef to develop menus and recipes for the restaurant. However, after a while Danielle realized that the lady was not producing the type of food offerings the people in Waco would be interested in eating. Therefore, she fired the chef and took over all the activities she had originally assigned to the chef. Danielle commented, "No one cares as much about a business as the entrepreneur, so I need to take over this very important position myself." During the first year of operation, Danielle found herself working about 80 hours a week at the restaurant and her job at Baylor.

Danielle found it difficult to find people who wanted to work hard. At first, she used Indeed and other employment sites, but none of them produced the type of hard-working employees that she wanted. Then she began asking a couple of her back-of-the-house employees, and they recommended people who worked well in the restaurant. She found that restaurant workers have a good network, and they can recommend good employees. The reason for the success of this method was that employees would not want to recommend someone who would not be a good employee because it would reflect poorly on them.

The new employees were paid $9.00 an hour, plus shared tips, and that amount was increased if they performed well and stayed with the restaurant. Danielle set up the restaurant as a hybrid of table service and counter service. When guests walked in the door, placed an order and paid for it, they were then invited to find a table to sit down and be served. Since the tips were given at the counter, Danielle split them with all employees. The employees who had been there since the beginning were making about $17.00 to $19.00 an hour by March of 2020.

Food Sourcing

Since Danielle had decided to feature farm-to-table offerings in her restaurant, she had to find an efficient source for those products. Therefore, she went to a food show and met several farmers from whom she bought farm products. Some of these were Urban produce for vegetables, Brazos Valley Cheese and Rosewood Ranches for beef. She also learned that working through a food broker would save her time and money so she secured Hardie's, a broker from Austin, to fill that position. She knew she paid more for the middleman, but it was worth the time it saved her. Danielle also decided that every ingredient she purchased had to be used in at least two food offerings. For example, when she used ciabatta bread for a sandwich, she would cut off the ends of the bread and use them as croutons. Her menu reflected the vocabulary of the church that had stood on this location for many years. (See Figure 8.2 entitled "Revival Restaurant menu.")

THE CORONAVIRUS PANDEMIC

In December of 2019, the first cases of COVID-19 were diagnosed in Wuhan, China. By January of 2020, the World Health Organization (WHO) declared the virus a Public Health Emergency of International Concern. Then on March 11, 2020, the WHO labeled the virus a "pandemic."[3] By June 1, the virus had been located in 188 countries and territories, and more than 372,000 deaths had been reported worldwide. The virus strain was identified as severe acute respiratory syndrome coronavirus 2 (SARS-CoV-2).

When the virus was declared to be a pandemic by the WHO, the leaders of most nations of the world immediately responded by closing all businesses except those deemed to be the most essential and setting guidelines for individuals that were labeled "social distancing." Citizens were asked to stay at home, if possible; and when they went out, to keep a 6-foot distance from other people, wear a mask and protective gloves. People were asked to prevent the spread of the virus by washing their hands as often as possible.

The United States government through the Small Business Administration (SBA) initiated a program called the Payroll Protection Program (PPP) to allow businesses to keep their employees on the payroll during the time that they were closed down. However, a business owner had to apply for the program and assure the SBA that the grant would be used solely for the purpose of retaining employees and paying for utilities, rent and mortgage interest. Any amount not forgiven by the government would be charged to the business with a 1 percent interest assigned. As long as a business used the loan for the stated purposes, it would be 100 percent forgiven.

By June of 2020, 40 million Americans had filed for unemployment compensation as the result of closed businesses due to the coronavirus pandemic. The country had not seen anything like this since the Great Depression. To help with the job losses, Congress passed a $2 trillion relief package which they called the CARES Act. This legislation included increased benefits for states who pay the unemployment compensation to their own citizens. The unemployment checks included an extra $600 per week through July 31, 2020, an increase in the number of weeks a person would be eligible for the benefits to 39 weeks and an inclusion in the bill for the self-employed and gig economy workers like Uber drivers.

SINGLE LOCATION RESTAURANTS IN THE U.S.

In 2016, annual spending on food at restaurants exceeded the money spent for groceries for the first time in U.S. history according to data from the U.S. Department of Agriculture. Consumer preferences for restaurants have been changing appreciably in the past five years. More consumers preferred to patronize local establishments which were oriented around a single chef or singular concept rather than large, homogenous chains with stale menu and décor concepts.[4] In addition, consumers are more inclined to select healthy and environmentally conscious food options and want to eat healthy, local produce.

In the spring of 2020, the food service sector took a hit by the COVID-19 pandemic. To retard the spread of the virus, many state governments ordered non-essential businesses, which included restaurants, to temporarily shutter. Thereafter, industry operators opted to indefinitely close their doors and offer take-out and delivery services amid the outbreak period. To help restaurants combat falling revenue, online delivery services announced that they would waive commission fees for restaurants during the pandemic period.

Many customers were still concerned about the safety of the take-out and delivery services as the virus was believed to last on plastic and cardboard surfaces for up to 72 hours. Some restaurants were unable to offer take-out and delivery because of the nature of their food. For example, steakhouses were unlikely to offer steaks to go as their foods need to be served hot.[5]

Baby boomers are a major group that influences industry revenue growth. Not only are they a very large percentage of the population, but they are the population with the greatest share of the nation's wealth. They also tend to have a higher level of disposable income, and the pressure of their jobs encourages them to eat out at restaurants more often. In addition, as millennials and the older members of Generation Z enter the workforce, they are more likely to spend money eating out. Although these generations tend not to have as much money as the baby boomers, they like smaller privately owned restaurants.

CRISIS MANAGEMENT

Crisis management is the process by which an organization deals with a disruptive and unexpected event that threatens to harm the organization or its stakeholders.[6] Normally, the managers of an organization have a short time in which to make a decision on how to confront and handle the crisis. Venette (2003, p. 7) suggests that "crisis is a process of transformation where the old system can no longer be maintained."[7] Therefore, for the crisis to be handled adequately, some type of change is normally required in an organization.

Erika Hayes James, an organizational psychologist at the University of Virginia's Darden Graduate School of Business, identifies two primary types of organizational crisis: A sudden crisis and a smoldering crisis. James defines organizational crisis as "any emotionally charged situation that, once it becomes public, invites negative stakeholder reaction and thereby has the potential to threaten the financial well-being, reputation, or survival of the firm or some portion thereof.[8] This researcher suggests that there are five phases of crisis that require specific crisis leadership competencies. These stages are: Signal detection, preparation and prevention, containment and damage control, business recovery and learning.[9]

The coronavirus pandemic occurred so quickly that businesses around the globe had to respond quickly in order to survive. The response of the organization was often shaped by policies of the federal, state and local governments in which the business was located.

THE DECISION

Danielle knew she had to make a decision rapidly in order to determine the future of her restaurant. For an organization that had been open less than a year, this was a critical decision. The employees she had in place (especially those in the back of house) had already become invaluable, and she hated to lose them. However, she wondered if she would be able to find some way to operate during the pandemic.

Figure 8.1   Exterior of Revival Restaurant

MENU

SANDWICHES

*ALL SANDWICHES SERVED WITH FRENCH FRIES;
UPGRADE TO SWEET POTATO FRIES OR BROCCOLI SLAW

WEIGHT OF GLORY
Portobello mushroom, caramelized balsamic onions, pesto aioli, arugula, fontina, broche bun

TECHNICOLOR DREAMCOAT.
Sweet potatoes, shredded and pickled beets with red onions, lemon garlic aioli, arugula, whipped herb goat cheese, multigrain bread

8TH DAY
Chicken, bacon, tomatoes, avocado, mayonnaise, bibb lettuce, cheddar, multigrain bread

OLD PESTOMENT.
Chicken, tomatoes, pesto, balsamic reduction, arugula, parmesan, ciabatta bread

PTL.
Bacon, tomato, bibb lettuce, lemon garlic aioli, rosemary sourdough bread

PRODIGAL SON.
Steak, caramelized balsamic onions, chimichurri sauce, mayonnaise, arugula, parmesan, ciabatta bread

RACHEL.
Roast beef (Certified Hereford Beefs), pickled red onion, horseradish aioli, arugula, cheddar, rosemary sourdough bread

LEAH.
Roast beef (Certified Hereford Beefu), caramelized balsamic onions, lemon garlic aioli, bibb lettuce, fontina, aabatta bread

TRINITY.
Fontina, provolone, cheddar, tomato, sourdough bread

SALADS

*SALADS CAN BE SERVED WITH YOUR CHOICE OF CHICKEN, STEAK, OR PORTOBELLO MUSHROOM.

EVE.
Roasted sweet potatoes and brussel sprouts, apple, dried cranberries, pumpkin seeds, cotija, kale, apple cider vinaigrette

SPURGEON.
Pickled beets and red onions, bacon, candied peanuts, goat cheese, arugula, bacon balsamic vinaigrette

RENDER UNTO CAESAR.
Parmesan, garlic croutons, baby kale and romaine, Caesar vinaigrette

GARDEN of EATING.
Corn relish (corn, serrano, red onion, cilantro), grape tomatoes, okra, queso fresco, baby kale, house vinaigrette

HOUSE SALAD.
Grape tomatoes, cucumbers, red onion, garlic croutons, romaine, ranch vinaigrette

EST · 2019
Revival
EASTSIDE ★ EATERY
WACO · TEXAS

BURGERS

*ALL SANDWICHES SERVED WITH FRENCH FRIES;
UPGRADE TO SWEET POTATO FRIES OR BROCCOLI SLAW

GOLDEN CALF.
Beef patty (Certified Hereford Beef), caramelized balsamic onions, whipped herb goat cheese, lemon garlic aioli, arugula, brioche bun

BUILD YOUR OWN.
Beef patty (Certified Hereford Beefs), brioche bun
SUBSTITUTE A PORTOBELLO MUSHROOM

TOPPINGS AT NO CHARGE
Tomatoes, red onions, white onions, pickles, mayonnaise, ketchup, dijon mustard, bibb lettuce, yellow mustard, arugula

EXTRAS ....PRICED
INDIVIDUALLY
Slice of bacon
Fried egg
Caramelized balsamic onions
Pickled red onions
Pickled red beets and onions
Sautéed portobello mushroom pieces
Sliced avocado

CHEESES ....PRICED
INDIVIDUALLY
Provolone
Fontina
Cheddar
Whipped herb goat cheese
American

HOUSE MADE SAUCES .... .25 EACH
Horseradish (1011, pesto aioli, garlic lemon aioli, chimichurri sauce, ranch vinaigrette

SIDES

FRENCH FRIES WITH HOUSE MADE SAUCE.

SWEET POTATO FRIES WITH HOUSE MADE SAUCE.

BROCCOLI SLAW.

OUR KITCHEN INCLUDES MANY GREAT INGREDIENTS LIKE, DAIRY, GLUTEN, AND NUTS. IF YOU HAVE FOOD ALLERGIES, PLEASE SPEAK WITH THE CASHIER ABOUT SPECIFIC MENU ITEMS AND WE WILL BE HAPPY TO PREPARE YOU SOMETHING SEPARATELY.
ASK ABOUT OUR VEGAN, GLUTEN FREE, DAIRY FREE AND NUT FREE OPTIONS!

KIDS

TITUS.
Grilled Amercan cheese sandwich on multigrain bread With french fries

PROMISED LAND.
Almond butter and honey sandwich on multigrain bread with french fries

BOARD OF
Kiddie charcuterie board - Pick 4 of our proteins, nuts, vegetables, and fruits
ASK THE CASHIER FOR THE DAILY SELECTION!

DRINKS

ICED TEA.

HOT TEA.

CRAFT SODA.

TOPO CHICO.

COFFEE FREE (FILLS.

NITRO COLD BREW COFFEE (ON

BEER (ON TAP AND BOTTLED)
Visit with bartender for current offerings

WINE.
Visit with bartender for current offerings

SWEETS

CHOCOLATE CHIP COOKIE.

CRAFT SODA
WITH VANILLA ICE CREAM.

NITRO COLD BREW COFFEE
WITH VANILLA ICE CREAM.

MOUSSE.
Ask cashier for flavor of the day

WE HOPE YOU ENJOY YOUR FOOD AS MUCH AS WE HAVE ENJOYED PREPARING IT!
A MAJORITY OF OUR MENU ITEMS ARE WHAT WE LIKE TO CALL 'TEXAS TO TABLE', WHICH MEANS FRESH PRODUCE, MEATS, CHEESES, AND EGGS ARE TEXAS-SOURCED WHEN POSSIBLE. ADDITIONALLY, WE HAVE CAREFULLY CRAFTED OUR MARINADES, DRESSINGS, SAUCES, AND RUBS IN HOUSE.
ALL COFFEE, SODA, AND BEER IS FROM TEXAS.

CONSUMING RAW OR UNDERCOOKED MEATS, POULTRY, OR EGGS MAY INCREASE YOUR RISK OF FOODBORNE ILLNESS

Figure 8.2   Revival Restaurant menu

NOTES

1. Young Life is a non-profit organization whose mission is "Introducing adolescents to Jesus Christ and helping them grow in their faith."

2. The buying and renovation of houses in deteriorated urban neighborhoods by middle-income professionals, thus improving property values but often displacing low-income families.

3. World Health Organization (June 1, 2020). Novel coronavirus 2019: Events as they happen. https://www.who .int/emergencies/diseases)novel-coronavirus-2019/events-as-they-happen/. Accessed May 28, 2020.

4. Le, Thi (April 2020). IBISWorld, US Industry Report 72211B.

5. Ibid.

6. Bundy, Johnathan, Pfarrer, Michael D., Short, Cole E. and Coombs, W. Timothy (2017). Crises and crisis management: Integration, interpretation, and research development. *Journal of Management*, 43, No. 6, 1661–1692.

7. Venette, S.J. (2003). Risk communication in a high reliability organization: APHIS PPQ's inclusion of risk in decision making. Ann Arbor, MI: UMI Proquest Information and Learning.

8. James, Erika Hayes (2008). Crisis leadership. https://ssrn.com/abstract=1281843/. Accessed June 3, 2020.

9. James, Erika Hayes (Spring 2007). Leadership as (un)usual: How to display competence in times of crisis. https://web.archive.org/web/20100705021756/ (http://www.leadershipreview.org/2007spring/Article4/pdf). Accessed June 3, 2020.

REFERENCES

Bundy, Johnathan, Pfarrer, Michael D., Short, Cole E. and Coombs, W. Timothy (2017). Crises and crisis management: Integration, interpretation, and research development. *Journal of Management*, 43, No. 6, 1661–1692.

James, Erika Hayes (Spring 2007). Leadership as (un)usual: How to display competence in times of crisis. https://web.archive.org/web/20100705021756/ (http://www.leadershipreview.org/2007spring/Article4/pdf). Accessed June 3, 2020.

James, Erika Hayes (2008). Crisis leadership. https://ssrn.com/abstract=1281843/. Accessed June 3, 2020.

Le, Thi (April 2020). IBISWorld, US Industry Report 72211B.

Venette, S.J. (2003). Risk communication in a high reliability organization: APHIS PPQ's inclusion of risk in decision making. Ann Arbor, MI: UMI Proquest Information and Learning.

World Health Organization (June 1, 2020). Novel coronavirus 2019: Events as they happen. https://www.who.int/emergencies/diseases)novel-coronavirus-2019/events-as-they-happen/. Accessed May 28, 2020.

9

Maintaining a business during a recession – Kleinfeld Bridal: absolutely "yes"!

https://www.kleinfeld.com/say-yes-to-the-dress/

In late March 2020, the owners of Kleinfeld Bridal posted the following notice on the store's "Appointments" page:

> Due to the uncertainty regarding the COVID-19 pandemic, we are currently accepting bridal appointments for May 16th and beyond but these appointments may need to be rescheduled based on government orders. Once the Governor of NY allows Kleinfeld to open, we will accommodate brides on a first-come, first-serve basis. If you would like to be notified of the earliest possible appointments, please click here to be added to our waiting list.

The pandemic had hit New York harder than any other state in the United States, and the citizens had been asked to practice social distancing and to "shelter in place" until the virus was under control. Kleinfeld, like many other retail clothing stores, could only wonder about the time New York and its businesses would reopen, how they should handle this difficult situation and what steps they should take to open at the end of the pandemic.

HISTORY OF KLEINFELD

Kleinfeld had been providing brides with dresses for 75 years (see Figure 9.1 entitled "Bridal dress"). In 1941, Hedda Kleinfeld and Jack Schacter of the Kleinfeld family, launched the company. Initially, the operation was a single storefront with three dressing rooms and featured the sale of furs and dresses for special occasions. The store would spend the next sixty years on Fifth Avenue in Bay Ridge, Brooklyn, which was considered a shopping haven for New York brides who wanted a personal touch. Later, the store would move to Chelsea in Manhattan. Then in 1968, Hedda Kleinfeld introduced the sale of wedding dresses designed by European fashion artists.

By 1979, the store expanded and discontinued the sale of furs and evening dresses to concentrate solely on wedding dresses. They offered over 400 styles and 12 dressing rooms. In 1990, the store was sold to Michel Zelnik and a group of venture capitalists. Then in 1996, the store was acquired by Gordon Brothers Capital. Then three years later, Mara Urshel, Ronnie Rothstein and the star of the *M*A*S*H* television program Wayne Rogers, bought Kleinfeld Bridal and increased the size of the store to include 18 dressing rooms and 13 fitting rooms.

In 2000, Mara Urshel expanded the retail selection of wedding dresses to include European dresses and designer exclusives. The inventory now reached a total of 800 dresses. In 2005, Kleinfeld related to its newly renovated location in Manhattan with 28 dressing rooms, 1,500 designer sample dresses, and a staff that now included 250 employees. Kleinfeld was now able to assist 17,000 brides a year in selecting a bridal gown.

Arguably the most important milestone for the company occurred in 2006 when the store began filming their bridal series *Say Yes to the Dress*. The program was shown on TLC (The Learning Channel). A sad event for the store occurred in 2015 when the president and co-owner of the store Wayne Rogers died.[1] Mara Urshel became president and as of 2020 was still serving as president of Kleinfeld.

BACKGROUND OF OWNERS

Mara Urshel

Mara worked for Saks Fifth Avenue for over 20 years serving as senior vice-president and general merchandise manager over divisions which represented 41 percent of Saks' total volume and 60 percent of Saks' total profit. She was responsible for the development and launching of many of Saks' private label brands as well as the introduction of several well-known designers including Donna Karan, Isaac Mizrahi, Michael Kors and Perry Ellis. Ms. Urshel believed in a hands-on approach to managing a business and could be found in the store most days. Her background proved beneficial in developing the private labels for Kleinfeld as well as identifying the new bridal designers and exclusives for Kleinfeld. One watching the television show *Say Yes to the Dress* would notice that she normally accompanies the main buyer, Dorothy, on buying trips and is well-respected in the apparel industry.[2]

Ronnie Rothstein

Ronnie graduated from the University of Pennsylvania and practiced law and held various management positions in the hospitality industry before going into investment banking. During the 1980s and 1990s, his investment firm specialized in business strategies and consulting. Ronnie, Mara and Wayne Rogers (of the *M*A*S*H* television show) bought Kleinfeld Bridal in 1999, and Ronnie has served as Kleinfeld's CEO since that time. Mr. Rothstein's background in management has also proved to be beneficial in the running of Kleinfeld as he, too, can be found in the store most days and believes strongly in customer service. He even gives his business card out with his phone number on it and tells the bride to contact him if there is ever an issue.[3]

INTERESTING FACTS ABOUT KLEINFELD

Appointments

There is no charge for an appointment for a bridal dress fitting at Kleinfeld, but a customer must reserve an appointment with a charge card. If a customer fails to cancel an appointment 48 hours before the appointment, she will be charged a cancellation fee of $100. The bridal consultant who assists the customer will bring somewhere between three to six dresses for the bride to try on based on the information the customer has furnished early such as fabric, cut and neckline. At any one time, Kleinfeld carries an average of 1,000 wedding dress samples by 60 designers from which the bride can order her size.

A standard wedding dress appointment at Kleinfeld normally lasts 1.5 hours, and the bride usually brings two to four people with her for the selection. There are anywhere from 25 to 30 bridal consultants (who wear solid black apparel) and 10 to 12 accessories consultants that work for Kleinfeld. The bride also can make an accessories appointment for consultation regarding a headpiece, veil, tiara, shoes, purse and jewelry.

Bridal Dresses

The average amount of money spent on a bridal dress at the store is $4,500. The most expensive dress that is normally in stock is a $32,000 ball gown by the designer Pnina Tornai. However, one of the Tornai designs did sell for $80,000. When the bride decides on a dress, the store erupts in cheers.

There are three alteration packages starting at $895 for the Signature Alterations Package which includes three fittings over a 2–3 month period.[4] Kleinfeld has the largest custom sewing workroom in the tri-state area and can accommodate 90 seamstresses, beaders, pressers and fitters. The second floor of the store was remodeled in 2019 and is home to bridesmaids' dresses, mother-of-the-bride/mother-of-the-groom dresses and flower girl dresses. This area is called Kleinfeld Bridal Party and has a separate website, www.kleinfeldbridalparty.com. The price points were lower for the bridal dresses carried at Kleinfeld Bridal Party and the bridesmaid dresses ranged from $129 to $299. During the COVID-19 pandemic, Kleinfeld had a statement on their Kleinfeld Bridal site that if a bride needed a dress or bridesmaid dresses in stock, they could go to the Kleinfeld Bridal Party site and purchase a dress from that site. Those dresses were in stock and would be shipped out within one day from a U.S. distribution center.

The Kleinfeld website features photos of diverse brides and bridesmaids, and many dresses can be ordered in sizes 2 to 32. In April 2020, the Disney Fairy Tale Weddings Collection was introduced with 7 of the 16 gowns being exclusive to Kleinfeld in the Platinum Collection ranging in price from $3,000 to $10,000. In addition to bridal dresses, bridesmaids' dresses and accessories, Kleinfeld also facilitates the blocking of hotel rooms in multiple cities for the bridal party.[5]

In an uncertain bridal market where some stores such as David's Bridal has faltered, Kleinfeld has stayed afloat. Two of the reasons for this are that the store has a commitment to customer service and a willingness to adapt to a modern era. In addition to the bridal gown, the store also has elaborate hairpieces, jewelry, shoes and even facilitates the rental of hotel rooms in Manhattan for the out-of-town brides. Fortunately, the store does have a Finance Department in case a bride needs financial assistance in paying for her gown.

The Men's Store

In 2010, Kleinfeld opened a clubby men's shop selling custom-made tuxedos and suits, just below its grand bridal salon at 110 West 20th Street (see Figure 9.2 entitled "Groom's attire"). Frank Jedda, the Director of Kleinfeld Men, suggested that he discovered men are often unaware of the basic tradition of formal attire. He commented, "Very often, they want to wear a tuxedo at 12 o'clock in the afternoon." Apparently, they were not acquainted with the tradition of never wearing a tuxedo before 6 p.m. The assortment of clothes for men includes morning coats, resort suits, shirt collars and neckties. A custom suit starts at $1,200.[6]

Pop-up Shop in New Jersey

In December of 2018, Kleinfeld launched a temporary pop-up shop in Secaucus, New Jersey. From January 3 to 13, brides were invited to shop the Kleinfeld shop at The Mall at Mill Creek, 31 Mill Creek Drive. The shop featured over 1,500 styles of designer wedding dresses including sample dresses and new over-stock items ranging in price from $199 to $899. These dresses normally ranged from $1,500 to $20,000. Kleinfeld co-owner, Mara Urshel, suggested:

> This is the first time in our 78-year history that our designer wedding dresses have ever been sold at these prices. In fact, no dress at the pop-up will exceed $1,000.[7]

Wayfair Revamped Dressing Rooms

In February of 2019, the online furniture store Wayfair Registry teamed up with the store to revamp two of the VIP dressing rooms—one of which was often featured in *Say Yes to the Dress*. The other dressing room is used for bridal appointments whether the brides are on the show or not. The revamped VIP dressing rooms provided new seating, wall art, new accessories and area rugs in calming color combinations from Wayfair Registry in order to create a more comfortable space while still keeping the focus on the bride as the previous dressing rooms had done.[8]

Say Yes to the Dress

The Learning Channel (TLC) developed and launched a television program labeled *Say Yes to the Dress* on October 12, 2007, based on the appointments brides-to-be attended at Kleinfeld's to pick out a bridal gown. The program followed the sales associates, managers and fitters of the store as a bride searches for the perfect dress.

The average episode drew approximately 1.3 million viewers. A blessing and a curse of the television program was that more people now knew about the store, but that made the store more crowded and often difficult to navigate for one who had come to select a dress.

Ronnie Rothstein, a Kleinfeld co-owner, suggested:

What the show has done for us is—it used to be an average of three people that come with the bride. Today, because of the show, they've got six, seven, eight people. There are no small bridal parties anymore.[9]

All of the brides for the show are cast well in advance of the taping; however, some brides come to their appointments hoping to get on the show. When entering the store, a guest is met with the following sign:

Please be aware that by entering Kleinfeld, you consent to your voice and likeness being videotaped and used without compensation for exploitation on television. If you do not wish to be on camera, please inform your sales consultant.[10]

The filming crew normally tries to shoot on Mondays, Tuesdays, Thursdays and Fridays. The program is shot in a 30,000 square foot showroom with white carpeting and $10,000 and up bridal gowns on mannequins. The backroom, which holds the dresses that customers will try on, has a large assortment of plastic-covered gowns that are organized by silhouette and designer. There are also hundreds of gowns hanging from the ceiling on a conveyor belt. The filmed appointment usually lasts about three hours whereas a normal appointment for a bride who will not be on the television program takes about an hour-and-a-half. Between the bride's pre- and post-interviews, there is a full eight to ten hours of filming to get one appointment shot according to Randy Fenoli, the star of the show and an independent consultant.[11] An interesting point is that Randy worked as Fashion Director at Kleinfeld's from 2007 to 2012 where he would consult with nearly 15,000 brides a year prior to being hired by TLC.[12]

TLC also launched multiple *Say Yes to the Dress* spinoffs including Atlanta (2010-2020), U.K. (2016-2017), England (2020), Australia (2016), Big Bliss (2010-2011), Northern Edition (2019-2020), and Randy Knows Best (2011-2014), Behind the Scenes (2018-2019), Wedding SOS (2018), and American (2019-2020).[13]

An interesting event that occurred shortly before the pandemic stopped filming was a special 10-episode series of *Say Yes to the Dress* that featured couples who represented every state, Puerto Rico and Washington, D.C. The event took place near the Bethesda Fountain in Central Park in New York City. Fenoli said of the series:

When you bring people together for a common purpose, which is love and marrying your partner, I think it's universal. I spent time with every single couple. And, as every single bride walked down the steps at Bethesda Fountain in Central Park, I announced her name and state as she met her groom, so they did have that individual moment.[14]

The last episode of this special series was shown on Friday, March 24, 2020, just about the time New York closed down for the pandemic.

BRIDAL STORES IN THE U.S.

Some of the trends that have affected bridal gown sales in the U.S. are the following:

- Rising disposable incomes have restrained industry revenue declines somewhat.
- A steadily declining marriage rate has hampered spending at bridal stores.
- Increasing competition from manufacturers and e-commerce has closed some operators.
- The coronavirus outbreak has stalled weddings and related spending in the short term.
- Bridal business is different from other retails during "social distancing" in that one cannot maintain six feet distancing during the initial appointment or the alterations fitting as it is very much a "hands on" type of business.
- Stores that leverage e-commerce and social media will have a better chance of competing.[15]

The top three companies with the largest market share are David's Bridal (300 stores), BHDLN owned by Anthropologie (21 stores) and Kleinfeld Bridal with just one store. The market size of the Bridal Stores Industry in the U.S. declined 2.2 percent per year on average between 2015 and 2020.

One of the major drivers of spending on bridal gowns is the marriage rate, and many consumers were choosing to postpone marriage as cohabitation outside marriage has grown in practice. Over the five years from 2015 to 2020, the marriage rate had declined at an annualized rate of 0.9 percent. Therefore, the revenue in this industry was expected to remain flat.

In addition, the median age at which people first get married climbed from 20 to 28 for women and from 23 to 30 for men between the years of 1960 and 2020.[16] However, as the median age of marriage for both men and women has increased, so has their disposable income. This has led to higher spending on weddings. One of the factors that has brought about higher incomes for women is the fact that in 1963 only 38 percent of women between the ages of 18 and 33 were employed. Whereas by 2020, 63 percent of millennial women were participating in the workforce.

In order to differentiate themselves from the growing online sellers, the traditional bridal store has sought to make itself unique by providing skilled salespersons who could upsell customers and increase revenue. In addition, many stores have sought to differentiate themselves by catering to an upscale or niche market as well as providing a better customer experience. IBISWorld suggests that this industry is in the mature stage of the product life cycle.

Over the 10 years leading to 2025, the industry's value added, which measures how much an industry contributes to the economy, was projected to decrease slightly and was expected to decline at an annual rate of 0.5 percent.

By the middle of 2020, the final impact of the coronavirus pandemic was unknown. However, in the early months of 2020, operators had already experienced a decline in revenues as they were forced by a government mandate at the federal, state, and local level to close their stores. An added problem for the stores was the fact that many weddings had either been canceled or postponed because of the "social distancing" mandate. It was also anticipated that more consumers would shift to online shopping because of travel restrictions.[17]

THE CORONAVIRUS PANDEMIC

The coronavirus was first diagnosed in Wuhan, China, on December 31, 2019. Initial research suggested that the disease had been spread through a lab in that city although the virus may have originated in an animal food market called a "wet market." The virus caused mild respiratory infections in about 80 percent of the individuals infected, and about half of them had pneumonia. Another 15 percent developed a severe illness, and approximately 5 percent needed critical care.[18]

By January 30, 2020, the outbreak was declared a Public Health Emergency of International Concern by the World Health Organization (WHO). On February 11, the WHO announced a name for the new disease: COVID-19. Then on March 11, the WHO declared the coronavirus a pandemic.[19]

On March 17, the United States and many countries of the world decided to require citizens to "shelter in place" in their habitations, and only the most essential of businesses were allowed to remain open. Unemployment grew rapidly, and soon economists began to speculate that the unemployment rate which had been around 3 percent in the United States might reach 20 percent. This was a level of unemployment unknown in the country since the Great Depression of the 1930s. Congress attempted to help individuals weather the pandemic with a check for $1,200 to every adult in the U.S. and $500 for each child under the age of 18. Under the Payroll Protection Program passed by Congress, businesses were invited to apply for a loan to keep their employees at work. The loan would not have to be repaid if the funds were used exclusively for payroll and either rent or mortgage to keep the business from going under.

CRISIS MANAGEMENT

Crisis management is the process by which an organization deals with a disruptive and unexpected event that has potentially serious consequences for an organization. The process normally goes through the following three stages: (1) Pre-crisis; (2) Crisis response; and (3) Post-crisis.[20] The pre-crisis phase would involve any actions that might be taken before a crisis occurs in order to minimize the effect of the crisis on the business. The crisis response stage entails the development of a plan for dealing with the crisis as quickly as possible. The post-crisis stage involves returning to business as usual. Steps involved at this point are such things as communicating the restoration of operations to all stakeholders and evaluating and developing a plan to deal with the effect of the crisis on the organization.

When it is perceived that a crisis will cause a disruption in business operations, a business continuity plan should be developed in an attempt to minimize the disruption. The first step is to identify the critical functions and processes that are necessary to keep the organization afloat.[21]

THE FUTURE

As the 17th of March, 2020, passed and businesses all over the U.S. began closing, the owners of Kleinfeld's Bridal looked at the future and began to speculate about what they should do while the nation was closed and when New York would begin opening again.

Figure 9.1   Bridal dress

Figure 9.2   Groom's attire

NOTES

1. Kleinfeld Home Page. https://www.kleinfeldbridal.com/say-yes-to-the-dress/. Accessed June 13, 2020.
2. https://www.kleinfeldbridal.com/kleinfeld-staff/. Accessed June 13, 2020.
3. Ibid.
4. www.kleinfeldbridal.com.
5. Ibid.
6. Wilson, Eric (June 16, 2010). For that other one in the photo. *The New York Times.* https://www.nytimes.com/2010/06/17/fashion/17ROW.html. Accessed May 28, 2020.
7. http://www.kleinfeldbridal.com/sale/. Accessed June 6, 2020.
8. McDowell, Maya (February 19, 2019). Wayfair Registry teamed up with Kleinfeld Bridal to revamp two of the VIP dressing rooms. *House Beautiful.* https://www.housebeautiful.com/design-inspiration/a26416660/wayfair-registry-kleinfeld-bridal-vip-dressing-rooms/. Accessed May 28, 2020.
9. Kleinfeld's harsh reality (2012). *New York Post.* https://nypost.com/2012/12/20/kleinfelds-harsh-reality. Accessed June 20, 2019.
10. Ibid.
11. Keegan, Kayla (January 5, 2020). Getting the Kleinfeld treatment was totally not what I expected. *Good Housekeeping.* https://www.goodhousekeeping.com/life/entertainment/a302561/say-yes-to-the-dress-randy-fenoli-kleinfeld-experience/. Accessed June 5, 2020.
12. https://www.kleinfeldbridal.com/designers/randy-fenoli/. Accessed June 18, 2020.

13. https://www.tlc.com/tv-shows/say-yes-to-the-dress/. Accessed June 15, 2020.

14. Cohn, Paulette (January 3, 2020). Randy Fenoli says the new *Say Yes to the Dress: America* is the show on steroids. *Parade.* https://parade.com/974661/paulettecohn/randy-fenoli-says-the-new-say-yes-to-the-dress-america-is-the-show-on-steroids/. Accessed June 5, 2020.

15. Fernandez, Cecillia (April 2020). IBISWorld, U.S. Specialized Report 0D4222 on bridal stores.

16. Ibid.

17. Ibid.

18. Branswell, Helen and Joseph, Andrew (March 11, 2020). WHO declares the coronavirus outbreak a pandemic. https://www.statnews.com/2020/03/11/who-declares-the-coronavirus-outbreak-a-pandemic/. Accessed June 6, 2020.

19. Ibid.

20. Institute for Public Relations (October 30, 2007). Crisis management and communications. https://instituteforpr.org/criss-management-and-communications/. Accessed June 6, 2020.

21. The Professional Practices for Business Continuity Management, Disaster Recovery Institute International CDRI, 2007. https://drii.org/resources/professionalpractices/EN/. Accessed June 2, 2020.

REFERENCES

Branswell, Helen and Joseph, Andrew (March 11, 2020). WHO declares the coronavirus outbreak a pandemic. https://www.statnews.com/2020/03/11/who-declares-the-coronavirus-outbreak-a-pandemic/. Accessed June 6, 2020.

Cohn, Paulette (January 3, 2020). Randy Fenoli says the new *Say Yes to the Dress: America* is the show on steroids. *Parade.* https://parade.com/974661/paulettecohn/randy-fenoli-says-the-new-say-yes-to-the-dress-america-is-the-show-on-steroids/. Accessed June 5, 2020.

Fernandez, Cecillia (April 2020). IBISWorld, U.S. Specialized Report 0D4222 on bridal stores.

https://www.kleinfeldbridal.com/designers/randy-fenoli/. Accessed June 18, 2020.

https://www.kleinfeldbridal.com/kleinfeld-staff/. Accessed June 18, 2020.

http://www.kleinfeldbridal.com/sale/. Accessed June 6, 2020.

https://www.tlc.com/tv-shows/say-yes-to-the-dress/. Accessed June 15, 2020.

Institute for Public Relations (October 30, 2007). Crisis management and communications. https://instituteforpr.org/criss-management-and-communications/. Accessed June 6, 2020.

Keegan, Kayla (January 5, 2020). Getting the Kleinfeld treatment was totally not what I expected. *Good Housekeeping.* https://www.goodhousekeeping.com/life/entertainment/a302561/say-yes-to-the-dress-randy-fenoli-kleinfeld-experience/. Accessed June 5, 2020.

Kleinfeld Home Page. https://www.kleinfeldbridal.com/say-yes-to-the-dress/. Accessed June 13, 2020.

Kleinfeld's harsh reality (2012). *New York Post.* https://nypost.com/2012/12/20/kleinfelds-harsh-reality. Accessed June 20, 2019.

McDowell, Maya (February 19, 2019). Wayfair Registry teamed up with Kleinfeld Bridal to revamp two of the VIP dressing rooms. *House Beautiful.* https://www.housebeautiful.com/design-inspiration/a26416660/wayfair-registry-kleinfeld-bridal-vip-dressing-rooms/. Accessed May 28, 2020.

The Professional Practices for Business Continuity Management, Disaster Recovery Institute International CDRI, 2007. https://drii.org/resources/professionalpractices/EN/. Accessed June 2, 2020.

Wilson, Eric (June 16, 2010). For that other one in the photo. *The New York Times.* https://www.nytimes.com/2010/06/17/fashion/17ROW.html. Accessed May 28, 2020.

10
Attaining long-term success – Magnolia and The Silos: sustaining rapid growth

http://www.shop.magnolia.com/

In April of 2020, Chip and Joanna Gaines of the former *Fixer Upper* television show, announced that the launch of their new television network would be delayed until the spring of 2021. The network would be a joint venture with the Discovery Channel and had earlier been scheduled to launch on October 4, 2020. The start date of the network was pushed forward because of the appearance of the coronavirus pandemic. The new Magnolia Channel was scheduled to take the place of the DIY Network. Since the end of *Fixer Upper*, the Gaines had continued to buy property in the Waco, Texas, area and plan several new ventures for the area at the same time that they were lining up programs for their new network. Some observers wondered if such rapid growth could be sustained.

BACKGROUND ON THE GAINES

Both Chip and Joanna graduated from Baylor University, but Chip was three years ahead of Joanna. Chip had majored in marketing and started several businesses while he was in school. Some of these businesses were a prepaid laundry service, a fireworks stand and multiple lawn care businesses. He played on the Baylor baseball team for a while, and what he really wanted to be was a professional baseball player, but that was not to be. Joanna had studied communications and wanted to be a broadcast journalist.

They didn't meet in college but instead in the automotive shop that Joanna's father owned. Chip came in one day for service on his vehicle and saw a picture of Joanna on the wall. He decided at that moment that he wanted to marry her. Later, when he came back to have his brakes worked on, he met her for the first time. On one of their first dates, Chip climbed up into a magnolia tree to get Joanna a flower. The magnolia tree was one of their favorites, so they later decided to name their business after that tree. On their first date, Chip was an hour and a half late. Joanna commented on her first impression of him on that date:

> This guy had no hair. I'd imagined he had hair under the baseball cap, but nope. Just stubble. And his face was weathered and flushed red like he'd been working outside in the

hot sun all day long. He was wearing a reddish-toned leather jacket, too, and I thought, *'Is this red guy even the same guy I was talking to at the shop?'* It turned out that Chip had shaved his head to support a friend of his who was battling cancer.[1]

After a couple of years of dating, the couple got married in 2003. Shortly after this, they began launching a series of ventures that finally led to the *Fixer Upper* television show on HGTV.

MAGNOLIA BUSINESSES

One of the first businesses the couple started was a venture which was engaged in "flipping" houses. This type of entrepreneurial endeavor involves buying houses, fixing them up and selling them for a higher price. After completing the first house, Joanna exclaimed:

> We painted over the wall paper, left the popcorn ceilings intact, and spent most of our bathroom renovation budget on double shower heads.[2]

Flipping houses provided part of the money they needed to launch another business, but they had to borrow an additional $5,000 to have sufficient capital.

Magnolia Market

This was their first retail business, and it was launched in 2003. The first day the company was opened, Magnolia had forty customers. While Joanna was serving in an internship in New York during college, she found herself enamored by many of the city's unique and beautiful little shops. These memories led to the opening of Magnolia Market on Bosque Boulevard. However, by 2006 the couple decided to close the shop so that they could concentrate on their construction business and raising their children. The building did not go unused but was used for their construction business from 2006 to 2014. At that time, they decided to reopen the Magnolia Market at that location. Before long, they had outgrown the space and had to relocate downtown to the Silos. Then in 2018, the original little shop opened to the public again as a place where a customer could buy slightly damaged goods at a discount.[3]

The Silos

On October 30 and 31, 2015, Chip and Joanna opened their biggest venture called the Silos. The location was at 5th and Webster in downtown Waco where two large, unpainted grain silos had remained empty for many years. When the couple took their plans to the City Council, they requested that they be allowed to keep the silos unpainted to preserve their historical look. After some debate on the subject, the Council agreed to let them keep the silos as they were. The City Council also agreed to reimburse the Gaines $650,000 in Tax Increment Financing Zone funds to build two blocks of sidewalk in front of the Silos. As time went on, the Gaines continued to add additional features to the Silos such as a bakery, a large play area for children covered by the former top of an old barn and a place where food trucks could park and feed the approximately 35,000 visitors who normally came each week. The Magnolia Bakery opened at 7:30 a.m. Monday through Saturday, and by 7:00 a.m. a long line of patrons was already waiting in line to buy the delicious cupcakes and cookies.

Most of the items in the Silos were home-design accent pieces and gift items. Some of those items and their prices are: Bud vases ($8 and up); antique-look signage (for example, a Bakery sign for $88); Magnolia Farms T-shirts ($26); kitchen canisters ($16); fancy soap ($12); picture frames ($8 and up); silk flowers ($9 and up) and Joanna's favorite candle which is $26.[4]

The popular Church Under the Bridge, hosted by Mission Waco, which had met underneath the I-35 Highway in Waco had to be relocated when construction began on repairing the highway. The church was then moved to the Silos for church on Sunday mornings when the market was closed. By 2019, around 1.5 million people a year were visiting the Silos. That was approximately the same number of people who visited the Alamo in San Antonio, Texas, each year. The Alamo had historically been considered the top attraction in the State of Texas. However, there was some criticism by other businesses in the city initially that the Silos and the large crowds gathering there was interrupting the traffic flow in downtown Waco. In response to that concern, the Gaines arranged for other parking areas and the City provided additional shuttles to carry people in the downtown area.

Other Ventures

Some of the other ventures the Gaines were involved in were:

1. An exclusive product line at Target called Hearth and Hand;
2. An online store;
3. An interior design company;
4. A wallpaper line;
5. A furniture line;
6. A paint line with Ace Hardware;
7. A line of designer pillows and rugs;
8. A best-selling cookbook; and
9. A couple of bed and breakfast locations.

One of those bed and breakfast locations was named the Magnolia House. The vacation home was located in McGregor which is a small town located approximately 20 miles from Waco. The Magnolia House began taking reservations for 2017 in February of 2016, and the facility was booked for the next year within minutes. The rate for the entire house was set at $695 a night, and guests were required to stay at least two nights. The house was large enough for a family reunion or other similar event.

Another creation of the Gaines was the Magnolia Table. The location of this restaurant was in the former Elite Café which could trace its founding back 97 years. It later became a popular stop for tourists traveling between Dallas and Austin before traffic moved to Interstate 35. One of the favorite stories of the Elite Café was that a young soldier named Elvis Presley ate there when he was stationed in the Army at Fort Hood nearby. However, when the traffic shifted to the Interstate, the Elite Café lost customers and finally had to close.[5] The Magnolia Table came into that location and served breakfast and lunch from Monday through Saturday. The

Meredith Corporation calculated that the *Magnolia Journal's* brand footprint which described the typical journal reader was the following:

> Then in 2016, the Gaines launched a lifestyle magazine called *The Magnolia Journal* which was published by Meredith (the *People Magazine's* parent company). The journal had a wide appeal, and the Meredith Corporation discovered that the typical reader had the following characteristics: Median income of $92,500; 81 percent owned their own home; 83 percent were married; 36 percent would be classified as millennials; 44 percent were parents; and the median age was 50.[6]

In addition, each spring they hosted a fundraising marathon, half-marathon and 5k run to support a worthy non-profit. The event was originally planned for the residents of Waco, but it soon began drawing people from all over the world.

Fixer Upper

In 2013, Chip and Joanna filmed the first episode of *Fixer Upper* for HGTV. On the first episode of the program, the couple transformed an "uninhabitable den for hoarders" into a beautiful home. The show was an instant winner, and the pilot had 1.9 million viewers. The show was renewed for five seasons with an option for a sixth. The network focused on buyers of homes in need of care that were transformed into dream homes. One of the concerns that Chip and Joanna had was whether the television program was taking them away from their children more than they wanted. Their four children and a fifth on the way were the most important part of their lives. Several weeks after the last episode was shown in 2018, the network aired a program entitled *Fixer Upper: Behind the Design* which gave fans of the program a never-before-seen look at their design secrets.[7]

After the last showing of *Fixer Upper*, Chip exclaimed:

> Jo and I can't believe we're watching the last episode of *Fixer Upper*. Who's watching with us? While we are confident this is the right choice for us, it has for sure not been an easy one to come to terms with.[8]

Some of the homes that the Gaines decorated during the five years that they were on HGTV could be viewed by the public. The couple had a strong following of fans who loved to see everything that they had done. The remodeled homes were private residences; and, therefore, they were not open for tours. However, some were available through AirBnB.com or VRBO. com for lodging. The homes within the City of Waco which had obtained licenses for people to be able to stay overnight could be found on the website http://www.wacoheartoftexas.com/lodging/. By 2019, a new business named Waco Tours (not owned by the Gaines) had been started, to show people around town and view some of those residences.

THE MAGNOLIA NETWORK

The new lifestyle-focused media network that had been proposed by the Discovery Channel for Chip and Joanna was projected to be launched on October 4, 2020. A spokesman for the Discovery Channel said of the proposal:

> Discovery is thrilled to confirm that we are in exclusive talks with Chip and Joanna Gaines. The Gaines are exceptional people with quality, family-friendly programming which will be accessible on a 24/7 network and across all screens.[9]

A subscription streaming service was set to debut later. Chip and Joanna were scheduled to take over the Discovery Channel's DIY Network which by 2019 reached more than 52 million homes. The Gaines' plans were to rename it the Magnolia Network. The network was projected to have programming focused on community, home, garden, food, wellness, entrepreneurialism and design.[10] (See Box 10.1 entitled "Proposed programs for the Magnolia Network.") However, because of the coronavirus pandemic in the spring of 2020, the launch of the network was delayed.

Chip announced the new channel during an appearance on *The Tonight Show Starring Jimmy Fallon* in November of 2018. At that time Chip commented:

> We signed a non-disclosure and it said quote unquote you can tell your Mother, but that's it. So, Mom, I just wanted to make a quick announcement, we are coming back to television. You are going to get to see the kids grow up. You are going to see us, well maybe a six-month delay like the rest of the world, but we are excited to be back.[11]

Discovery was the owner of HGTV after its $12 billion purchase of Scripps Networks. The DIY Network was the home of Clint Harp's *Wood Work* series. Harp originally gained national and international attention as the carpenter who made many of Joanna's creations for their *Fixer Upper* program.[12]

COFFEE SHOP

In April of 2019, the Gaines announced that they had purchased property located a block away from the Silos in downtown Waco to launch a coffee shop. The early plans for the shop included a full-service coffee bar, fresh-baked pastries and an assortment of teas. A takeaway window and both indoor and outdoor seating areas were planned.[13]

CHALLENGES FOR FIRMS

Hisrich et al. suggest that there are both advantages and disadvantages for firms experiencing rapid growth.[14] Some advantages are economies of scale, attractiveness to suppliers and increased perception of legitimacy to customers. However, there are a number of potential challenges that a rapidly growing firm may face. A few of these are the following:

1. Pressure on Human Resources

With the added workload that often comes with growth are such employee problems as stress, burnout, depression and higher turnover. With an influx of new employees, the company may discover that the corporate culture has been appreciably altered.

2. Pressure on Management of Employees

For an entrepreneur who has managed all of the employees of the company from the beginning, rapid growth may present difficult challenges. It is often hard for the founder to realize that the human resource management situation has gone beyond his or her ability to lead.

3. Pressures on the Entrepreneur's Time

Time is a precious and limited resource for everyone—but especially for the entrepreneur who is growing a business quickly. Work/life balance may be critically disabled and the entrepreneur may face decisions about time that can never be appropriately redressed.

4. Pressures on Existing Financial Resources

Often the strain on limited resources may lead to an early demise for the firm. That is perhaps the most challenging physical aspect of growing a firm. There have been many instances of firms that filled a void market niche, had an outstanding product or service, and yet grew faster than their financial assets would allow and had to file for bankruptcy. The sad element of the failure was that committed customers were without a product or service for which they had grown fond.

THE FUTURE OF MAGNOLIA FARMS

With such an amazing rate of growth, Magnolia Farms must look at the future and determine what, if any, additional offerings are in order. The challenge of the new television network will certainly take first place in the deliberations of the Gaines, but they must also have a strategy for managing existing products and the possible introduction of new offerings.

BOX 10.1 PROPOSED PROGRAMS FOR THE MAGNOLIA NETWORK

- "Home on the Road" – a look at family life for Johnnyswim duo Amanda and Abner Ramirez and their children.

- "Growing Floret" – about the organic Floret Flower Farm in Washington State.
- "Restoration Road" – featuring Waco woodworker Clint Harp as he looks at building restorations across the country.
- "Family Dinner" – with host Andrew Zimmern visiting families to see how food brings people together.
- "Super Dad" – with comedian and host Taylor Calmus joining other dads in building elaborate projects for their kids.
- "Bespoke Kitchens" – about kitchen remodeler/furniture maker deVOL Kitchens of Leicestershire, England.
- "Home Work" – Andrew and Candis Meredith's project to convert a 113-year-old schoolhouse into their nine-member family's dream home.

Source: Hoover, Carl (April 22, 2020). Gaineses to tease Magnolia Network in 4-hour weekend preview. *Waco Tribune-Herald*, 1st page, below the fold.

NOTES

1. Yang, Lucy (January 3, 2018). Everything you need to know about the real-life love story of "Fixer Upper" stars Chip and Joanna Gaines. *Insider*. Accessed July 30, 2019.

2. Gaines, Joanna (n.d.). Instagram. Accessed May 6, 2018.

3. Magnolia website. https://www.magnolia.com/little-shop-on-bosque/. Accessed July 29, 2019.

4. Dumenco, Simon (December 22, 2015). 10 things you need to know about Chip and Joanna Gaines' Magnolia Market. http://www.countryliving.com/life/travel/news/a37149/10-things-chip-joanna-gaines-magnolia-market/. Accessed August 5, 2019.

5. Copeland, Mike (May 10, 2016). Magnolia buys historic Elite Café. *Waco Tribune-Herald*, Local Section, p. 1.

6. www.meredith.com/brand/themagnoliajournal/. Accessed June 20, 2018.

7. Chip and Joanna Gaines's emotional "Fixer Upper" farewell (April 4, 2018). Gale Academic Onefile. http://link.galegroup.com/apps/doc/A533264073/AONE?u=txshracd2488&sid=AONE&xid=89523a39. Accessed July 29, 2019.

8. Respers, Lisa (April 4, 2018). Chip and Joanna Gaines; emotional "Fixer Upper" farewell. *CNN Wire*. Accessed July 30, 2019.

9. Stein, Megan (November 10, 2018). Discovery just released more details about Chip and Joanna Gaines' new TV network. *Country Living*. https://www.countryliving.com/life/entertainment/a24929146/chip-joanna-gaines-discovery-new-tv-network. Accessed July 29, 2019.

10. Bradley, Laura (April 10, 2019). How Chip and Joanna Gaines traded *Fixer Upper* for a network of their own. *Vanity Fair*. https://www.vanityfair.com/hollywood/2019/04/chip-and-joanna-gaines-own-network-discovery-fixer-upper/. Accessed February 7, 2021.

11. Strohm, Emily (November 10, 2018). Chip & Joanna Gaines are returning to TV with their own Discovery Network: Excited to be back! *People Magazine*. https://www.people.com/home/chip-joanna-gaines-tv-network-return-to-television/. Accessed December 10, 2018.

12. Hoover, Carl (April 11, 2019). Gaines reveal more on TV deal. *Waco Tribune-Herald*, Local, p. 1.

13. Magnolia to branch out with downtown coffee shop (February 19, 2019). *Waco Tribune-Herald*, Local, p. 1.

14. Hisrich, Robert, Peters, Michael and Shepherd, Dean (2019). *Entrepreneurship*, 11th edition. New York, NY: McGraw-Hill Education.

REFERENCES

Bradley, Laura (April 10, 2019). How Chip and Joanna Gaines traded *Fixer Upper* for a network of their own. *Vanity Fair*. https://www.vanityfair.com/hollywood/2019/04/chip-and-joanna-gaines-own -network-discovery-fixer-upper/. Accessed February 7, 2021.

Chip and Joanna Gaines's emotional "Fixer Upper" farewell (April 4, 2018). Gale Academic Onefile. http://link.galegroup.com/apps/doc/A533264073/AONE?u=txshracd2488&sid=AONE&xid= 89523a39. Accessed July 29, 2019.

Copeland, Mike (May 10, 2016). Magnolia buys historic Elite Café. *Waco Tribune-Herald*, Local Section, p. 1.

Dumenco, Simon (December 22, 2015). 10 things you need to know about Chip and Joanna Gaines' Magnolia Market. http://www.countryliving.com/life/travel/news/a37149/10-things-chip-joanna -gaines-magnolia-market/. Accessed August 5, 2019.

Gaines, Joanna (n.d.). Instagram. Accessed May 6, 2018.

Hisrich, Robert, Peters, Michael and Shepherd, Dean (2019). *Entrepreneurship*, 11th edition. New York, NY: McGraw-Hill Education.

Hoover, Carl (April 11, 2019). Gaines reveal more on TV deal. *Waco Tribune-Herald*, Local, p. 1.

Hoover, Carl (April 22, 2020). Gaineses to tease Magnolia Network in 4-hour weekend preview. *Waco Tribune-Herald*, 1st page, below the fold.

Magnolia to branch out with downtown coffee shop (February 19, 2019). *Waco Tribune-Herald*, Local, p. 1.

Magnolia website. https://www.magnolia.com/little-shop-on-bosque/. Accessed July 29, 2019.

Respers, Lisa (April 4, 2018). Chip and Joanna Gaines; emotional "Fixer Upper" farewell. *CNN Wire*. Accessed July 30, 2019.

Stein, Megan (November 10, 2018). Discovery just released more details about Chip and Joanna Gaines' new TV network. *Country Living*. https://www.countryliving.com/life/entertainment/a24929146/chip -joanna-gaines-discovery-new-tv-network. Accessed July 29, 2019.

Strohm, Emily (November 10, 2018). Chip & Joanna Gaines are returning to TV with their own Discovery Network: Excited to be back! *People Magazine*. https://www.people.com/home/chip-joanna -gaines-tv-network-return-to-television/. Accessed December 10, 2018.

www.meredith.com/brand/themagnoliajournal/. Accessed June 20, 2018.

Yang, Lucy (January 3, 2018). Everything you need to know about the real-life love story of "Fixer Upper" stars Chip and Joanna Gaines. *Insider*. Accessed July 30, 2019.

11

Exploring new business – Lily Jade: developing an online apparel business driven by social media

https://www.lily-jade.com

In May of 2020, Meggan Wood looked over the variety of upscale diaper bags she had created for her company, Lily Jade, and wondered what the next step in the business should be. Eight years ago, she and her husband, Landon, had created this company, and they were pleased that it had been so profitable. All of Lily Jade's operations had been online thus far, and she wondered if they should consider other methods of operation.

BACKGROUND ON THE WOODS

Landon was truly a born entrepreneur. When he was eight years old, he opened his first business. He had gone to the bank and borrowed some money to buy a lawnmower and edger to begin his own lawn care business. Landon surmised that he was the only eight-year-old he knew who had a bank account and a balance sheet.

He was always starting businesses. While he was studying entrepreneurship and international business at Baylor University, he started a tree trimming business and made enough money to get married and have a fabulous honeymoon. Landon called this business Wood's Tree Surface. He and Meggan moved to San Antonio, Texas, and would often go knocking on doors with flyers for his tree trimming business.

After several years of operation, Landon launched a pewter cross business. He found a factory in Mexico that would mold the crosses and then pour pewter into the molds. A problem arose with this business when the demand for his products grew so rapidly that he could not find sufficient cash to fund the operations. Larger department stores like Dillard's wanted such large quantities of his product that he found it impossible to meet the orders. He discovered that large companies such as this would not normally pay their suppliers for 90 days. His next venture was a successful biomedical research instrumentation company that was profitably acquired after two years of strong growth.

LAUNCHING LILY JADE

When their first child was about to be born, Meggan found that she didn't like any of the diaper bags on the market and decided to design her own. She wanted a bag that could also pass as a regular tote later. She envisioned that the bag would have a pouch inside that would hold everything she needed for the baby. Later when she no longer needed a diaper bag, she could remove the pouch and have a classy leather handbag. This bag would be a departure from other diaper bags at the time which were usually produced in bright colors and loud patterns.

Then in 2011, Landon sold his instruments business and spent time contemplating the next business to launch while working on the side as a product development consultant. Because of Meggan's interest in developing a more fashionable diaper bag, Landon decided to research that industry. After extensive market research, he concluded that if they produced fashionable leather diaper bags with a removable pouch, there would be a market niche for their product.

An Imposter

In October of 2012, Meggan and Landon launched their diaper bag company. They decided to go exclusively with e-commerce to sell their bags. Meggan named the company Lily Jade after her niece, Lily, and her Mother's preference for jade jewelry. Since they would be using social media to sell their products, Meggan felt she would at last be able to use her communications and journalism majors from college. However, neither of them knew how to talk about leather and leather construction. In addition, an obstacle for Meggan was that she felt like an imposter because she didn't know the market or how to sketch or sew.

The Sourcing King

Meggan soon began calling Landon "The Sourcing King" because he was able to find the right resources that they needed for their business. At first, Landon looked for a seamstress who made tote bags on Etsy. He asked the woman to sign a non-disclosure agreement that contained a picture of her envisioned diaper bag. Landon knew they needed to find someone who could do the technical drawing for the bag so he went online through LinkedIn where he found a consultant who had worked for Vera Bradley and other designers. After the consultant refined the design, a factory was identified that could take the design, crate samples, and begin production (see Figure 11.1 entitled "Lily Jade diaper bag"). This consultant was invaluable in teaching Meggan how to talk the language of the industry. Landon's name as "The Sourcing King" was earned by asking questions that should have embarrassed him to people in the industry out of complete ignorance. He had decided that was the only way to learn the intricacies of this industry.

The leather in their bags came from cow hide sourced primarily from North and South America. The finishing process was carried out at a tannery in New York. The hides were a by-product of the beef industry.

Operating in China

The couple moved production of their bags to China because labor was too expensive in the United States. They had originally produced the bag in the U.S., but taking the production to China reduced the costs by 66 percent. Additionally, they enhanced the quality of their product in China. They had attended a trade show in Hong Kong and found their producer in China. They chose this particular company because the owners shared the Wood's ethical business beliefs, and it had been a family run business for over 20 years. This company hired artisans who were experts in their craft, and they paid higher wages in order to recruit and retain quality craftsmen.

Meggan found that for high-end brands, the best quality was in China. Landon had talked to the factory which also produced Coach handbags, and they said they did not have the skill set to make the product the couple wanted because of the complexity in the design. The couple found that if they followed the Chinese rules, there would be no problem with the loss of intellectual property. They learned that if they had a problem, they could get an attorney in China to protect their brand.

The Woods believed that their biggest competition came from two upstart American brands competing in the millennial mom space. The design of the bags produced by these companies was similar to the Woods' bags, but they were made out of faux leather and carried a cheaper price tag.

Filling Orders

When they began their operations, the Woods stored their products in the garage and filled the orders themselves. That became too cumbersome and time-consuming, so they found a fulfillment operation in Atlanta, Georgia. By 2020, they had added another fulfillment company in Austin. The fulfillment operations not only helped to reduce their shipping costs, but also handle any surge in purchases of their products. All of the returns were handled in-house in their San Antonio facility. The process they established for returns was: Inspect, grade and document issues for possible resale or reclassify for no sale. Some of the items were put in outlet classification. The Woods established a 30-day return/exchange policy to accept a returned product as long as the original bag was in new/unused condition.

Using Social Media

The Woods primarily used Instagram, Facebook ads as well as social influencers. They found that the most difficult part of this was learning to use the language of social media. Once they had learned how to master this, they found that their competition would take their words and use them. They found they could trademark their slogan, and it would be harder to reproduce. (See Box 11.1 entitled "Lily Jade's social media" and Box 11.2 entitled "Social media analytics.") By 2014, the couple had assigned some people on their team to concentrate on social media and the identification of those who were stealing the descriptions of their products. In 2015, they had a shipment of bags to Mexico that was copied. Their employees did an Instagram post about it, and that stopped further copying from that particular company.

In order to analyze the conversion rate of their website, they used Google Analytics, data from their shopping carts and Facebook ad measurements. They found that all of these played an important part. They also used tools for monitoring and evaluating the performance of their Ambassador Program which was composed of bloggers and influencers. They had discovered that 8 to 10 percent of their sales were outside the United States. Those sales were primarily from Canada, Australia and the United Kingdom.

Meggan and Landon also held "meet and greet" events which were similar to "pop-up shops." They would share on their social channel that they would host events in certain cities and invite people to come and have coffee with them. They took bags along with them to these events in case some of the guests wanted to buy a bag. By 2020, they were holding several of these events each year in various cities and states. They found that this kind of event was more common in the social space. Their competition had also begun hosting similar events.

Employees

By the spring of 2020, the company had a mix of 15 full- and part-time employees. The employees handled such operations as customer service, supply chain and human resource management. They had one employee who handled their social channels and campaigns.

INDUSTRY OUTLOOK

The closest industry that is relevant to Lily Jade is the Online Baby Products Sales Industry. Ibisworld.com stated there was an annualized market size growth of 9 percent between 2015 and 2020. The U.S. market size in 2020 was $9.3 billion and the growth in sales was expected to be 7.6 percent in 2020.[1] The industry had benefitted from a growing acceptance by consumers of online shopping. Competitive pricing and more multichannel retailing options had fueled this growth.

Ibisworld.com suggests that some of the key external drivers of the industry are an increase in disposal income, growth in e-commerce sales, increase in the number of broadband connections, and rising birth rates around the world. However, one of the challenges to small companies has been the high level of discounting of prices by large retailers. The industry is expected to mature over the years leading up to 2024 due to intensified competition and e-commerce becoming even more of a part of the mainstream shopping culture in the U.S. Further innovations in online shopping platforms are expected to give parents more convenient options for purchasing these products.

Approximately 250 Key Success Factors are tracked by Ibisworld.com for any business. They have suggested that the most important success factors for this industry are the following: The ability to quickly adopt new technology, provision of superior after-sales service, having a loyal customer base, the ability to control stock on hand, meeting safety standards and a good reputation.[2]

LOOKING TO THE FUTURE

Although the Woods' sale of products exclusively on the internet had been successful, they wondered if they were remiss in not considering other retail avenues. They had an initial introduction to supplying large department stores when they were producing the pewter crosses. Although that did not work out for them, they had a stronger cash flow situation by 2020 and might be able to carry receivables on their books longer.

They also considered the fact that selling their products through department stores or maternity shops could greatly increase the scope of their operations. They wondered what factors they should evaluate in deciding on a future course of action.

Figure 11.1   Lily Jade diaper bag

BOX 11.1   LILY JADE'S SOCIAL MEDIA

Lily Jade Website
Captured on April 19, 2019
https://www.lily-jade.com/pages/our-story

During my first pregnancy, I desired to maintain my style along with the need to be organized.

With limited diaper bag options, I chose a well-known designer tote and loaded it with Ziplock bags full of baby essentials…but there had to be a better way.

I wanted a bag to carry precious memories beyond the baby years. I envisioned rich leather, plush materials, and a well-organized design. Being comfortable toting baby essentials or a laptop on a light was a priority.

I dreamed of a bag that could work at a play date or a dinner date. Deciding that I didn't need a different bag for everything I do.

I began to design one bag that could do it all and look good doing it.

Lily Jade was created for this.

Company giving:

Your diaper bag dollars go the distance to help moms all across the globe.

Lily Jade believes in elevating the life-giving, more-challenging-than-you-ever-imagined, glory filled role of motherhood.

We partner with Embrace Grace to provide loving and practical resources for women with unplanned pregnancies. Hosting baby showers is one of the many ways Lily Jade connects you to these ladies.

Your investment helps moms you may never meet, clothe a baby you may never kiss and creates hope and lasting friendships that nurture hearts for a lifetime.

Your Lily Jade purchases bless families committed to adoption! This is dear to our hearts and we are passionate about championing the women involved in this path.

Birth mothers, foster mothers and adoptive mommas need us to cheer them on! Because you shop at Lily Jade, we can regularly bless these families through charitable contributions, giveaways and community support.

BOX 11.2   SOCIAL MEDIA ANALYTICS

Sixty percent of the world's population (internet users are aged 16 to 64) are spending an average of 6 hours and 43 minutes each day online. Of that, they are spending an average of 2 hours and 24 minutes on social media across all devices each day.[3]

Apps account for 90 percent of total time spent on mobile activities with social media accounting for half of the time spent on mobile devices.[4]

As of April 2020, the most popular social networks worldwide ranked by number of active users: #1 Facebook (2.5 billion monthly active users with 170 million mobile app users); #2 YouTube (1.8 billion monthly active users); #6 Instagram (1 billion monthly active users with 121 million mobile app users); #13 Snapchat (398 million monthly active users with 46 million mobile app users); #14 Twitter (386 monthly active users with 81 million mobile app users); #15 Pinterest (366 monthly active users with 67 million mobile app users).

The engagement with shoppable Product Pins on Pinterest increased 44 percent from 2019 to 2020. Searches increased 60 percent year over year from the months between March and June 2020 (during the quarantine period from COVID-19).[5]

One study showed consumers are almost 14 times more likely to be influenced to purchase a product by a peer rather than a celebrity, proving the strength of online influencers.[6]

Because of the growing use of social media, businesses have begun to gather and evaluate the large amount of data now available about customers' or potential customers' feelings about their products of services. The new field created to evaluate this wealth of information is called social media analytics (SMA).

SMA uses analytics capabilities in order to generate specific types of knowledge such as gathering intelligence/staying informed, detecting potential problems/opportunities, making sense of that opportunity, coming up with insights, and making business decisions.[7]

Methods of Applying SMA

There are three primary methods of applying SMA. These three are: (1) Text analysis or mining; (2) social network analysis; and (3) trend analysis. Krippendorff suggests that "Text analysis/mining is a research technique within the field of content analysis that supports researchers in making replicable and valid inferences from texts to the contexts of their use."[8]

Social network analysis looks at the relationships between people, organizations, interest groups, states, and so on by evaluating the structure of their connections.[9] So, in this context, SMA can identify some of the opinion leaders or influencers in a particular product category.

Trend analysis utilizes recent advances in technology to apply algorithms to the data that has been gathered to predict certain trends in an industry.

Stages of Capturing and Using Data

SMA normally takes place in three stages: Capture, understand and present.

"Capture involves obtaining relevant social media data by monitoring or 'listening' to various social media sources, archiving relevant data and extracting pertinent information."[10] The understand stage involves attempting to assess the meaning of the data the organization has captured and evaluating the application of that data to the organization's operations. This is the heart of SMA. Finally, in the present stage, all of the results of the data collection are summarized and evaluated and then presented to the people in the organization who can make use of the analytics.[11]

Growth of SMA

Marketandmarkets.com suggests from its research that the global social analytics market will grow from $1.6 billion in 2015 to $5.4 billion in 2020 at a compound annual growth rate of 27.6 percent. North America is the leading revenue-generating region for SMA and Europe follows.[12]

NOTES

1. Ibisworld.com. Online baby product sales in the US market size 2002-2025. https://www.ibisworld.com/industry-statistics/market-size/online-baby-product-sales-united-states/. Accessed June 21, 2020.

2. Ibid.

3. 2020 Global Digital Overview. https://datareportal.com/?utm_source=Statista&utm_medium=Data_Citation_Hyperlink&utm_campaign=Data_Partners&utm_content=Statista_Data_Citation. Accessed June 23, 2020.

4. Most popular social networks worldwide as of April 2020 ranked by number of active users. *Statista*. https://www.statista.com/statistics/272014/global-social-networks-ranked-by-numer-of-users/. Accessed June 22, 2020.

5. Smith, Sandy (May 25, 2020). Through the retail lens: Social marketing and retail. *National Retail Federation*. https://nrf.com/blog/through-retail-lens-social-marketing-and-retail/. Accessed June 22, 2020.

6. Pianalto, Brooke (October 14, 2019). How to meet your target market under the mistletoe. *Marketing Dive*. https://www.marketingdive.com/spons/how-to-meet-your-target-market-under-the-media-mistletoe/564649/. Accessed June 22, 2020.

7. Holsapple, Clyde W., Hsiao, Shih-Hui and Pakath, Ram (March 13, 2018). Business social media analytics: Characterization and conceptual framework. *Decision Support Systems*, 110, 32-45.

8. Krippendorff, K. (2004). *Content Analysis: An Introduction to its Methodology*. London, UK: Sage Publications, p. 4.

9. Scott, J. and Carrington, P.C. (2011). *Handbook of Social Network Analysis*. London, UK: Sage Publications.

10. Fan, Weiguo and Gordon, Michael D. (June 2014). The power of social media analytics. *Communications of the ACM*, 57, No. 6, 74-81.

11. Ibid., p. 77.

12. Marketandmarkets.com (2016). Social media analytics market worth $5.4 billion USD by 2020. http://www.marketandmarkets.com/PressReleases/social-media-analytics.asp. Accessed June 22, 2020.

REFERENCES

2020 Global Digital Overview. https://datareportal.com/?utm_source=Statista&utm_medium=Data_Citation_Hyperlink&utm_campaign=Data_Partners&utm_content=Statista_Data_Citation. Accessed June 23, 2020.

Fan, Weiguo and Gordon, Michael D. (June 2014). The power of social media analytics. *Communications of the ACM*, 57, No. 6, 74-81.

Holsapple, Clyde W., Hsiao, Shih-Hui and Pakath, Ram (March 13, 2018). Business social media analytics: Characterization and conceptual framework. *Decision Support Systems*, 110, 32-45.

https://www.lily-jade.com. Accessed April 19, 2019.

https://www.lily-jade.com/pages/our-story/. Accessed April 19, 2019.

Ibisworld.com. Online baby product sales in the US market size 2002–2025. https://www.ibisworld.com/industry-statistics/market-size/online-baby-product-sales-united-states/. Accessed June 21, 2020.

Krippendorff, K. (2004). *Content Analysis: An Introduction to its Methodology*. London, UK: Sage Publications.

Marketandmarkets.com (2016). Social media analytics market worth $5.4 billion USD by 2020. http://www.marketandmarkets.com/PressReleases/social-media-analytics.asp. Accessed June 22, 2020.

Most popular social networks worldwide as of April 2020 ranked by number of active users. *Statista*. https://www.statista.com/statistics/272014/global-social-networks-ranked-by-numer-of-users/. Accessed June 22, 2020.

Pianalto, Brooke (October 14, 2019). How to meet your target market under the mistletoe. *Marketing Dive*. https://www.marketingdive.com/spons/how-to-meet-your-target-market-under-the-media-mistletoe/564649/. Accessed June 22, 2020.

Scott, J. and Carrington, P.C. (2011). *Handbook of Social Network Analysis*. London, UK: Sage Publications.

Smith, Sandy (May 25, 2020). Through the retail lens: Social marketing and retail. *National Retail Federation*. https://nrf.com/blog/through-retail-lens-social-marketing-and-retail/. Accessed June 22, 2020.

12
Starting a social enterprise – The TLC Rocket Stove: results-based financing through carbon credits

http://www.totallandcare.org

Jordan Kowalke had a deep concern about the difficult and dangerous life of women in Malawi (and most of Africa) who had to search two or three days a week for wood to use in cooking their food on an open fire. He expressed his anxiety in this way:

> I am trying to help Malawian women rid their lives of drudgery. The act of collecting firewood, cooking on an open fire with the wind ripping through the site makes cooking many times longer. When they go for wood, they may be gone two to three hours a day several days a week. This is a dangerous, time-consuming task; and the women are exposed to many dangers. They're exposed to wildlife that may harm or kill them, to the possibility of sexual assault and the nature of the work itself. Carrying all this wood, sometimes bare-footed, is treacherous and devastating to a woman's body.

His company, Total Land Care, had developed a cookstove that would heat the food faster, using less wood and putting less carbon into the air. It was the fall of 2019, and Jordan had just seen a report that indicated his company's efforts to achieve 100 percent adoption of the stove had fallen short of their goal. Only a little over 70 percent of the villagers were now using the stove. He wondered how they could get the remainder of the villagers to use their stove knowing how it would improve their lives and help the environment.

COOKING IN AFRICA

For thousands of years, the people of most countries in Africa had been cooking their meals on an outdoor stove that was composed of three stones and a pot. Over 90 percent of the population had cooked with biomass.[1] In the urban environments, that biomass was charcoal. In the rural environments, most people cooked with wood. However, most of the charcoal production was from natural forests which caused a growing deforestation[2] problem. Another problem of the traditional cookstove was that it was very inefficient and used a large amount of biomass. Cooking over an open fire was the most expensive way to cook with wood, and rural households in sub-Saharan Africa dedicated 3.3 hours to 4 hours per day harvesting biomass energy.[3]

Throughout the world, over 3 billion people have relied on traditional fuels such as charcoal, dung, wood and agriculture residues.[4] In 2000, the total global production of wood reached 3.9 billion cubic meters of which 2.3 billion cubic meters was used for fuel. Therefore, approximately 60 percent of the world's total use of wood from forests and trees was used for energy purposes.[5]

In addition to the inefficiency and high cost of cooking with wood on the traditional stove, inefficient biomass-burning methods of cooking also had caused serious health issues such as elevated concentrations of inhalable particulate matter and stove-related respiratory illnesses with women and children at the greatest risk. Some of these respiratory illnesses were lung cancer and obstructive pulmonary disease. In addition, cooks had reported burns to the hands and lower arms and burning eyes from cooking on an open fire.

In order to provide wood for cookstoves, villagers had to concentrate on reforestation. However, there were several things competing with tree planting, and food production was the primary competitor for land use. If a natural forest was available, it became difficult to get people to plant trees and reforest the land.

BACKGROUND ON JORDAN KOWALKE

Jordan Kowalke grew up in Washington state and went to the University of Washington, obtaining a degree in marketing and communications. After graduation, he had several jobs in marketing—mostly in television. However, he knew rather quickly that this was not how he wanted to spend his life. He left his job in marketing and ran a restaurant for about 12 years. The business was community-based and near a university. It was in that setting that he met many graduate students, and some of them were from developing countries. After he had left the restaurant business, he started a craft business. He had always been interested in engineering and construction, and he became a cabinet maker catering to wealthy individuals.

After several years of this business, Kowalke became disillusioned with building furniture for wealthy people and became interested in organizations that were philanthropy-based. His desire shifted to building things for poor people. He wanted to use the skills he had to transfer some of the wealth from the U.S. to poorer countries and especially transfer technology.

Kowalke was especially interested in cookstoves because he believed that was low-hanging fruit as far as technology was concerned. This interest led him to work for a non-profit organization in Oregon called Aprovecho Research. This group was a world leader in cookstove design, cookstove testing and innovation. While he was with this organization, he began doing consultancies in Kenya, Malawi and Haiti. As a result of one of those consultancies, he secured a position with Total Land Care (TLC). TLC wanted Kowalke to manage their national stove program in Malawi for them.

TOTAL LAND CARE (TLC)

Total Land Care (TLC) was developed as a non-governmental organization (NGO) in Malawi, Mozambique, Zambia, and Tanzania by three friends. One of the friends was Trent Bunderson, an American, who had formerly been a professor at Washington State University. Another friend was Zwide Jere, a Malawian. After leaving his post at Washington State University, Trent had gone to Malawi and raised his family there. It was in Malawi that he met and became friends with Zwide and the third partner, Ian Hayes. Later, TLC was registered in Switzerland as TLC Global to diversify funding opportunities. TLC was founded to sustain and expand the successful agricultural and natural resource management programs of a 12-year project funded by United States Agency for International Development (USAID).

The men were concerned about some of the problems that plagued Malawi such as overpopulation and deforestation. The organization carried out a number of interventions to address the problems of the people of the targeted countries.

TLC Interventions

Interventions that were promoted and supported by TLC were jointly planned with targeted communities in an attempt to improve the lives of villagers through improvements in food security, nutrition, health and incomes. The TLC interventions were the following:

1. Forestry – To reduce deforestation and to supply forestry products to households;
2. Sustainable agricultural practice – To improve food security, nutrition and incomes;
3. Development of rural-based enterprises – To increase rural incomes; and
4. Water and sanitation – To reduce the incidence of common diseases.

Mission

TLC's mission was to improve the livelihoods and standards of living of smallholder farm households across the region.

Program Design and Implementation

This involved a community-based approach to addressing the basic needs and challenges that were identified by the targeted communities. This included such things as low agricultural production, food insecurity, poor nutrition, vulnerability to variable weather and climate change, limited access to capital, credit, markets, high incidence of common diseases, increasing shortages of wood for fuel and building needs, and degradation of natural resources.

Organization and Employees

The type of organization utilized by TLC was developmental consulting. There were 250 employees of the organization in 2019, and each one was involved in carving out its mission by collaborating with communities to conduct a needs assessment and evaluate land-use practices, crops, and livestock which would be best suited to those communities. After this, the organization developed community-based action plans that involved various interventions to address different needs.[6]

The organization's primary expertise was in tree nurseries and tree planting. However, in an attempt to preserve the existing forests, TLC developed a stove program that would use less charcoal and wood. They soon discovered that if you have a natural forest available, it is hard to get people to plant new trees. Since it takes approximately five years to get a tree to yield, Malawians often feel that valuable land should only be used for annual food crops—either cash crops or food crops for subsistence living.

Since TLC was an implementer with an expertise in tree planting, sovereign donors such as Norway, the United States, Ireland, Sweden, and the United Kingdom provided funding for TLC to implement development programs. The reason for this was that TLC had regional expertise in best practices for the types of development work that sovereign donors wanted to see happen. The donors wanted to see food security increase. They also wanted to see people cooking with cleaner technologies and more afforestation.[7]

One way that TLC envisioned those goals being accomplished was by the development of a cookstove that would reduce the use of charcoal and wood and preserve the forests. TLC encouraged the Malawians to develop their own wood lots, plant nurseries where they started trees from seed and plant trees each year. Concurrently with these afforestation efforts, TLC had introduced an innovative cookstove that used less fuel. This cookstove was called the "TLC Rocket Stove."

THE ROCKET STOVE

The rocket stove was an innovative type of cookstove developed by Aprovecho in about 2002. Since that time, it had become a standard, low-level, efficient, cookstove used all over the world. For example, China had many models of rocket stoves made of metal, and the United States had a number of companies making this type of stove and selling them to survivalists. No one had received a patent on this model of cookstove, so it was an open-source concept.

The original cookstove used by most Africans was simply three rocks with a pot on top with the fire burning beneath it. The rocket stove increased the efficiency of the traditional cookstove. One way to compare ways of cooking was a formula that was determined by the use of an index called "thermal efficiency." Thermal efficiency referred to the amount of energy in the fuel that is transferred into the pot and the food that was being cooked. The open fire was typically recognized to have a 10 percent thermal efficiency. Therefore, 90 percent of the energy in the fuel being used was wasted. Most rocket stoves had a thermal efficiency of about 20 percent. TLC discovered that they could utilize a metal device to surround the pot that would improve the heat transfer from the stove to the cook pot to a thermal efficiency of 28 to 30 percent. (See Figure 12.1 entitled "The Total Land Care rocket stove.")

From 2013 to 2016, there had been over 100,000 stoves installed in Malawi. Of these, 64,000 were funded by private investors. The remainder were funded by sovereign donors. The villagers were taught how to assemble their own rocket stoves by TLC. In 2017, another

Source: Total Land Care Malawi. *Energypedia.* https://energypedia.info/wiki/File:TLCRS.jpg. Accessed February 7, 2021.

Figure 12.1   The Total Land Care rocket stove

30,000 stoves were built utilizing carbon offset credits paid for by various sovereign donors such as USAID, the Royal Norwegian Embassy (RNE), Britain's Department for International Development (DID), the International Fund for Agricultural Development (IFAD), the European Union and the Food and Agricultural Organization (FAO). So, the program could be funded by either private investors or sovereign donors hoping to slow down deforestation in Africa by the utilization of stoves that were more efficient and used less wood than the traditional cooking stoves.

The private sector provided funds to TLC to implement social responsibility programs. These private funds came from such organizations as the Coca-Cola Company, Altria Group, Philip Morris International, Japan Tobacco, and the Foundation for Eliminating Child Labor in Tobacco. Some, but not all, of the stoves installed by TLC were associated with carbon credits.

If a sovereign donor agreed to use carbon offset credits to fund a TLC project, they would not choose to receive the proceeds but rather require TLC to reinvest in the communities served by the initial investment or donation. However, private investment groups did seek returns through the sale of carbon credits which were generated by the installation or maintenance of emission-saving technologies such as the rocket stove. The buyer of the carbon credits knew that these credits were of high quality because of the monitoring by an agency of the United Nations.

CARBON OFFSET CREDITS

Carbon credit markets had been developed to reward those who reduced their own greenhouse gas emissions below regulatory levels or those who captured carbon at a rate beyond "business as usual" to offset others' greenhouse gas emissions. These carbon markets could be either mandatory or voluntary. The voluntary markets were set up as a way for businesses to practice corporate social responsibility. Voluntary carbon credits could be purchased to satisfy either one's personal objectives or some corporate standard. These markets were in operation for 10 years before the regulatory compliance markets and were a testing ground for that system.[8]

The regulatory markets were developed to respond to the carbon emissions goals set by the United Nations Framework Convention on Climate Change including the 1997 Kyoto Protocol and the Paris Agreement of 2015.[9] There were a number of different regulatory markets around the world that allowed for the use of carbon offset credits. In other words, for an organization producing carbon emissions beyond the limits of the regulatory standard, the framework was available for that organization to buy excess carbon credits from an organization that was producing less than the required level of carbon emissions.

It was this system of carbon offset credits that allowed investment by organizations into the TLC development project. It was a results-based finance model; and donors, whether voluntary or mandatory, found that to be a very attractive way to handle their funds or to put their funds into development. One thing that had plagued programs in developing nations for many years was that donors became exhausted about giving money for good causes and not having any results obtained. With the carbon offset program, investment in a project happened initially; and then there was an opportunity for the investor to get a return from the certified carbon credits. There were a variety of methodologies for certifying the carbon credits. The one that TLC participated in was called the Clean Development Mechanism (CDM), and this operation was regulated by the United Nations. In regard to this operation, Jordan suggested:

> If you can come out on the other end with certified UN carbon credits, there's a good chance that the sovereign donors will buy the carbon credits for you; and in some cases, they will guarantee that they will buy them if you succeed.

In explaining the mechanism for the utilization of carbon credits, Jordan made the following statement: (See Figure 12.2 for the "Project model for carbon.")

> A carbon manager would put together a number of different parties. The manager would want to select organizations that might want to buy carbon credits as a social responsibility, whether those are sovereign nations or large corporations, whether those are voluntary or mandatory because of something like the Kyoto Protocol which made it mandatory that

certain nations bought carbon credits. More commonly now carbon credits are involved in a voluntary market or organization. The reason for that is that the Kyoto Protocol and the Paris Agreement of 2015 have lost a great deal of support.

In addition to international programs, there were state programs such as the one that existed in California which required that if an organization was going to build a structure in the state, they had to offset their carbon footprint by securing certified carbon offset credits. Also, under the Paris Agreement on carbon emissions, airlines were mandatorily required to buy carbon offset credits.

The way in which carbon offset credits affected TLC was if they could cut fuel use and emissions by 50 percent by securing the use of the rocket stove by Malawians, that could be quantified and proven in a lab setting. For example, if there were 100 TLC rocket stoves in use, then X amount of carbon per hundred stoves could be saved. In addition, it could also be shown that the operation of one stove could save a certain amount of carbon per year and produce carbon offset credits. In calculating the cost of carbon offset credits, one ton of carbon was equal to one carbon offset credit. It was an elaborate formula that determined this offset, and that formula was agreed upon by the United Nations. For the rocket stove, it had been found that one stove would save 2.6 tons of carbon going into the atmosphere per year. In explaining the price of carbon credits and how they were calculated, Jordan explained:

> If the initial investor invested $5.00 per stove; and you were able to get $5.00 per carbon credit, then in that first year the investor would have an $8.00 profit because 2.6 times 5 is 13. There is a yearly rigorous verification process to calculate this formula. The investors in this project have to pay for the third-party verifiers to come and examine the CDM methodology.

RESULTS-BASED FINANCING

The traditional model for development had been the donation of money for a specific cause; and in many cases, nothing ever happened. There was nothing to show for the donation at the end of the project. Often the money was inefficiently managed or corruptly absorbed. A problem was that most development assistance processes were focused on inputs rather than outputs and outcomes.

The disbursement was often tied to expenditures on inputs such as road building materials rather than miles of road built or transport time reduced. Or funds may have been allocated for school buildings and teacher recruitment rather than learning outcomes of the children. Because of a disenchantment with this method of development, a newer model of development investing called results-based financing (RBF) has undergone experimentation. Through this mechanism, the disbursement of funds has been more closely linked to outputs and outcomes rather than inputs.[10]

RBF has been applied differently in various contexts and sectors, and below is a partial list of some commonly used abbreviations and formats:

- **Cash on Delivery Aid (COD Aid)** is an approach that offers a fixed payment for each additional unit of progress toward a commonly agreed goal, e.g. $200 for each additional child who passes a standardized test at the end of primary school.
- **Program-for-Results (PforR)** was introduced by the World Bank in 2012 as a new lending instrument. This program links the disbursement of funds directly to the delivery of pre-defined results.
- **Out-put Based Aid (OBA)** links the payment of aid to the delivery of specific services or "outputs." These can include connection of poor households to electricity grids or water and sanitation systems.
- **Conditional Cash Transfers (CCTs)** use financial incentives in relation to individuals or households to encourage the use of certain services, like sending children to school or using preventive health services.[11]

In commenting on this newer method of funding development projects which was being used by TLC, Jordan commented:

Results based financing eliminates the buyer's need to monitor the funds it has dedicated to donating to developing countries and allows them to be assured of a successful program. Results based financing can theoretically privatize development work because it can produce revenue for an investor or can incentivize adoption of prudent technologies in a community.

CHALLENGES TO ADOPTION

Although the TLC Rocket Stove was designed from the bottom up (meaning: by local cooks during initial planning and design sessions), new technologies do not always appeal to every possible user; and the issue becomes an adoption issue that requires attention and often nuanced problem solving.

Efforts to achieve cookstove adoption must initially address multiple factors such as technical specifications, design, quality, accessibility, and an enabling environment. Jordan suggested that those factors are the following:

1. The technical specifications of the stoves used in the intervention had to actually meet the goals of improved efficiency and reduced emissions;
2. A requirement is that the product be desirable to the end user in terms of utility, cultural appropriateness, aesthetics, and perceived improvement over the old stove. This usually required tailoring the stove design for the general target audience. Investing upfront in market research and applying a user-centered approach to the design of the stove helped ensure the development of a final product that users were motivated to accept. If the stove provided tangible benefits, such as reduced fuel costs, faster cooking and health benefits, the household has an incentive to adopt the stove.

3. The stove also had to be durable; many users were in remote locations where the breakdown of a stove would simply result in its being discarded, which would harm the stove program's reputation. Post-acquisition support was needed such as repairs and a warranty and follow-up with users' needs. The availability of stoves and stove parts in local markets and the ease of installation and use in the home were very important to keep customers engaged—the ultimate benchmark for a sustainable market. Local metal workshops manufactured the cookstove parts as a core part of their business.

4. To ensure a dynamic cookstove community adoption, the traditional authority had to actively support the technology and support the concept of using less fuel and releasing less emissions.

THE PROBLEM

It was now the Fall of 2019, and Jordan Kowalke wondered how he could increase the percentage of villagers in Malawi who adopted the rocket stove from 70 percent to as near 100 percent as possible. He had found that in areas where farmers are "fuel poor," adoption of the stove was close to 100 percent. However, in areas where wood is not scarce, adoption had often been much lower. This left an average adoption rate of 70 percent. Jordan pondered whether the "Diffusion of Innovation" model he had studied at the university would have any answers for him (see Box 12.1 entitled "The Diffusion of Innovation"). Some of the methods he considered were the following:

Finding the innovators in each village and selling them on the idea of adopting the rocket stove;

Giving demonstrations of the stove at village meetings and involving local leadership. Jordan had discovered that the traditional authorities' skills as a leader or his or her investment, in the project either made or broke adoption rates;

Working with the Ministry of Agriculture through its Extension Department to distribute information about the stove; and

Providing seedlings for their land to villagers who adopted the technology to help with reforestation of the country while providing technology that would cut down on the use of wood.

Jordan wondered which one of these tools or which combination would work best in getting this new type of cooking stove into as many homes as possible.

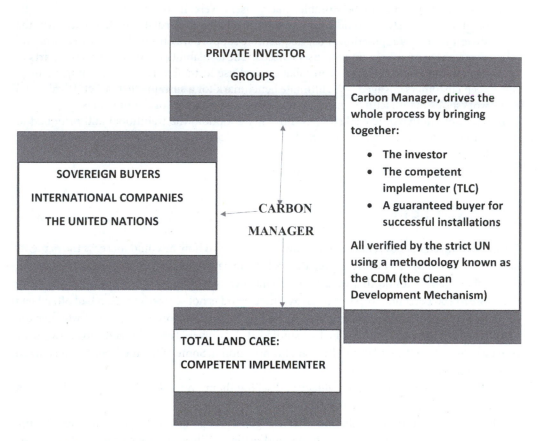

PRIVATE INVESTOR GROUPS

Carbon Manager, drives the whole process by bringing together:

- The investor
- The competent implementer (TLC)
- A guaranteed buyer for successful installations

SOVEREIGN BUYERS

INTERNATIONAL COMPANIES

THE UNITED NATIONS

CARBON MANAGER

All verified by the strict UN using a methodology known as the CDM (the Clean Development Mechanism)

TOTAL LAND CARE:

COMPETENT IMPLEMENTER

Figure 12.2   Project model for carbon

BOX 12.1   THE DIFFUSION OF INNOVATION

In 1962, E.M. Rogers developed a theory entitled "Diffusion of Innovation". This theory was an attempt to answer the question of how a new product gains momentum and spreads through the economy. The term "adoption" suggests that a person does something differently than what they had done before. This includes purchasing products that they had not purchased in the past. Researchers who have worked with this theory have developed a set of characteristics that they believe define people at each stage of the adoption process. Those stages and personal characteristics are the following (see Figure 12.3):

Innovators – People who are the first to try out a new innovation. These people are adventurous and interested in new ideas. It takes very little promotion to get these people to adopt a new product.

Early Adopters – These people are normally opinion leaders. They like the role of a leader and look forward to the opportunity to change. They need little information to cause them to adopt a new product.

Early Majority – These people are normally not leaders, but they do adopt a product before the average person does. They usually need to actually see the innovation work before they will adopt it. The top of strategies that appeal to this group are success stories from others that the product does what it says it will do.

Late Majority – This group of people are skeptical of change. They will not adopt a product until it has been successfully adopted by the Early Majority. The best strategy to win them over is evidence of how many people have already adopted the product successfully.

Laggards – These are very conservative people and are often bound by tradition. They are extremely skeptical of change and are the hardest consumers to bring on board. The best strategies to bring them aboard would be statistics of products purchased and pressure from people in the other adopter groups.

Organizations selling an innovative product, often try to find the opinion leaders in a particular category in order to get them to buy the product. They know that if they can get opinion leaders to buy, the other potential buyers may eventually be won over.

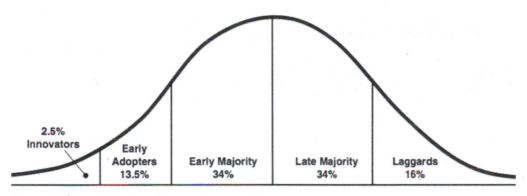

Figure 12.3   Diffusion of innovation model

NOTES

1. Biomass is a term used by the wood industry for getting energy by burning wood and other organic matter.
2. The action of clearing a wide area of trees.
3. The World Bank (2011). *Household Cookstoves, Environment, Health, and Climate Change*. Washington, DC: The International Bank for Reconstruction and Development, p. 13.
4. Bruce, N., McCracken, J., Albalak, R., Schei, M.A., Smith, K.R., Lopez, V. (2004). Impacts of improved stoves, house construction and child location on levels of indoor air pollution exposure in young Guatemalan children. *Journal of Exposure Analysis and Environmental Epidemiology*. Nature Publishing Group, 14, S26–533.
5. FAO. http://www.fao.orcp/copyright-en.htm.
6. Total Land Care Home Page. http://www.totallandcare.org/. Accessed July 19, 2017.
7. The establishment of a forest or stand of trees in an area where there was no previous tree cover.

8. Adoption of carbon credit programs among SFI participants in Maine (March 2017). The University of Maine, Center for Research on Sustainable Forests, p.4.

9. Ibid, p. 4.

10. O'Brien, Thomas and Kanbur, Ravi (April 10, 2013). The operational dimensions of results based financing. Research Paper, Cornell University Press.

11. *Results Based Financing Approaches—What Are They?* (2015). Stockholm: Swedish International Development Cooperation Agency Project for Results Based Financing.

REFERENCES

Adoption of carbon credit programs among SFI participants in Maine (March 2017). The University of Maine, Center for Research on Sustainable Forests, p. 4.

Bruce, N., McCracken, J., Albalak, R., Schei, M.A., Smith, K.R., Lopez, V. (2004). Impacts of improved stoves, house construction and child location on levels of indoor air pollution exposure in young Guatemalan children. *Journal of Exposure Analysis and Environmental Epidemiology.* Nature Publishing Group, 14, S26-533.

FAO. http://www.fao.orcp/copyright-en.htm.

O'Brien, Thomas and Kanbur, Ravi (April 10, 2013). The operational dimensions of results based financing. Research Paper, Cornell University Press.

Results Based Financing Approaches—What Are They? (2015). Stockholm: Swedish International Development Cooperation Agency Project for Results Based Financing.

The World Bank (2011). *Household Cookstoves, Environment, Health, and Climate Change.* Washington, DC: The International Bank for Reconstruction and Development, p. 13.

Total Land Care Home Page. http://www.totallandcare.org/. Accessed July 19, 2017.

Total Land Care Malawi. *Energypedia.* https://energypedia.info/wiki/File:TLCRS.jpg. Accessed February 7, 2021.

13

The role of a first mover – *The Fleet Sheet:* seeking sustainability for a first mover

http://www.fleetsheet.cz

At precisely 8:00 a.m. on Friday, October 18, 2019, faxes began printing out simultaneously in the offices of English-speaking companies all over the Czech Republic. Among the news of the Czech Republic translated into English that day was an interesting political insight gleaned from two newspapers:

> We normally don't delve deeply into pornography and steamy gossip, but this time it's necessary. We'll keep it short and to the point and provide some links for those who want more of the juicy details. Michaela Krausova, 27, resigned yesterday as head of the Pirates' caucus at Prague City Hall (but not as an assemblywoman) after being caught in a situation similar to that of Monica Lewinsky, except that Krausova was the politician this time.

It was this kind of honest, straightforward evaluation of the Czech economy, government and society that had made *The Fleet Sheet* so popular to foreign companies and their managers. Erik Best, the founder of *The Fleet Sheet*, had become an important political commentator in the city and was well known for his insightful articles. By the fall of 2019, Erik found that there were many decisions to be made concerning the future of the company as well as his own future.

ERIK'S EDUCATION AND EARLY WORK EXPERIENCE

Erik was born in North Carolina; and when he was 11 years old, his family moved to Montana. He went to high school there and wrote for the high school newspaper. He also became a part-time staff sportswriter for the *Missoulian*—the local newspaper. Near the end of his senior year in high school, Erik was offered a journalism scholarship to Vanderbilt University; however, he turned it down because at that time he was not sure he wanted to be a journalist. In the back of his mind, he had thought for some time that he wanted to be involved in business or politics or perhaps both. He decided to attend Georgetown University, and he received a degree in Foreign Service from Georgetown University in 1985.

In the summers while working on his undergraduate degree at Georgetown, he also studied the Russian language at Middlebury College in Vermont; a school well known for its concentration on international affairs. He subsequently received a master's degree in Russian from Middlebury in the Summer of 1985. Perhaps the educational experience that had the greatest impact upon Erik's life was a required four months' stint in Moscow. When he had completed his degree at Middlebury, he entered the M.B.A. program at the University of North Carolina at Chapel Hill and received his M.B.A. degree in 1987.

THE MOVE TO PRAGUE

Erik Best, a fluent speaker of the Russian language and one conversant in other Slavic languages, became enamored with the historic changes taking place in Eastern Europe. Never in the 20th century had the opportunity existed to be a part of such a great transformation. Never before in history had countries formerly living under a socialist government with centrally planned economies tried to make the transition to a free market economy where Adam Smith's "Invisible Hand" would be responsible for moving resources into their most advantageous usage.

Therefore, when the offer was made to Erik by the M.B.A. Enterprise Corps to join them in their work in Czechoslovakia, he quickly accepted. In February of 1991, Erik packed his bags and moved to Prague. He immediately fell in love with the country and found the Czech language very similar to Russian. In explaining his love of Prague to others, Erik would state:

> I have always loved music, and there is no city in the world so rich with music as Prague. There are classical concerts daily in concert halls, churches, town squares, on the breathtaking Charles Bridge, private chambers, large public halls and under street arches. There are violinists and accordionists playing on street corners and in Metro (underground) stations. I have heard that there are more musicians per capita in the Czech Republic than anywhere else in the world. After all, it was in Prague that Mozart wrote the opera "Don Giovanni" and found greater acclaim than in his own Austria. It was also the home of composers Dvorak and Smetana. This is one of the reasons I feel at home in this city.

ORIGINATION OF IDEA FOR *THE FLEET SHEET*

After working in Prague for a year, it became clear to Erik that international companies that had established offices and operations in the Czech Republic had difficulty in obtaining accurate and timely information on political and economic trends in the country upon which to make business decisions. From his work as a management consultant, he knew that decision makers in companies were very busy, and those operating in the Czech Republic would need information that was very concise and written in English. At the time, no such product was available in the country. It occurred to him that a one-page faxed bulletin would be the best format for such a paper. The fax was also an inexpensive medium to use. He knew that in the beginning there would not be much news to report, and a one-page sheet of paper would probably hold all he needed to print.

By early 1992, he had worked out all of the details to begin the business; and on February 22 he published the first issue. Erik believed that if he had four or five subscribers in the first month, the product would be successful. In fact, approximately 15 to 20 subscribers signed up in the first month of operations. By the fall of 2019, there were still a sufficient number of subscribers to make the business profitable.

Believing that the life cycle of his product would be relatively short, Erik took little thought to establishing a permanent structure for his business. He set it up as a sole proprietorship and did not bother with a business plan since the operations of the company were uncomplicated and easy to establish.

By 2019, Erik had a relatively small number of staff members in the company. Some of the staff came in the very early morning to review newspapers and begin translating the news from Czech to English. Other members of the staff came in around 7:30 a.m. and were involved in distribution and client support.

Erik assumed the major responsibility for picking out the most important news to be translated and distributed in *The Fleet Sheet*. He believed a key competitive advantage of *The Fleet Sheet* was its emphasis on a quality product that reported useful Czech economic and political news. Occasionally, the *Sheet* had made a person unhappy by interpreting something incorrectly. However, if Erik agreed with the person's argument, he would admit it and print a retraction. He had found it important to listen to customer complaints and recognize the needs of the customer. He attempted to treat his readers as equal partners. The name for his paper came from the fact that it was issued in a timely manner, and also in reference to Fleet Street in London where all of the major newspapers once resided before moving to the Docklands.

THE SITUATION IN EASTERN EUROPE

In the early 1990s, the break-up of centralized socialist economies was occupying all over Eastern Europe. Simultaneously, there was a rapid growth of the private sector in Russia and the surrounding countries of Poland, Czechoslovakia and Hungary. One of the challenges in the burgeoning market economies was creating small businesses out of large enterprises and also launching entirely new ventures where none had been before.[1] In fact, the development of the small business sector had been the most successful manifestation of the movement to a market economy. Small businesses had also been the greatest success story in the privatization process. Auctions of small businesses and the restitution of property in these countries had led to the restoration of some family businesses.

However, numerous problems beset these newly created companies. In some cases, the venture was merely additional work added to one or two other jobs to keep the entrepreneur afloat with increasingly higher inflation rates and increasingly stagnant wage rates. Many small businesses were forced into operating illegitimately to deal with unfair and cumbersome legal procedures in the regulatory environment, or to avoid the attention of the Mafia or corrupt officials. It became very difficult to work out a secure contract for lease of property, and the banking system was not equipped to deal with the needs of small business.

Another serious problem was the lack of experience in running private businesses that existed in Eastern Europe. Most hopeful entrepreneurs had lived all of their lives in a socialist economy and had no training or knowledge related to the way in which one becomes an entrepreneur. It was into this environment that many organizations from the West sent consultants to assist with the revitalization of the economy as a free market. The M.B.A. Enterprise Corps was one such operation.

THE PRICING STRATEGY

Erik realized immediately that the major publication constraint would be the number of people he could physically fax copies of *The Fleet Sheet* to in a short period of time. This was primarily due to the fact that he knew there would be a limitation on the number of telephone lines that he could get. He also knew that another constraint was the budget of the companies and when they needed to have the news. The larger multinational companies, he speculated, would be willing to pay a higher price to get the information very early in the morning. On the other hand, smaller companies beset with fewer complicated decisions would probably be willing to pay a lower price to have the information later in the day. Some businesses might need the information only once a week.

On the basis of this assessment, Erik constructed a pricing structure that averaged $3 to $4 per day for the customer who wanted *The Fleet Sheet* faxed to him or her early in the morning; and for the smaller companies who needed *The Fleet Sheet* faxed to them only once a week, the price would drop to $.50 to $.75 an issue. There would be intermediate pricing between the two end points. Therefore, the large companies and lawyers for whom "time is money," could have access to all of the Czech political and economic news early in the morning so that they could make astute and timely decisions based upon realistic information. The companies that did not need information in a timely manner could enjoy the benefit of a discounted price for the information. The graduated pricing strategy would also make the distribution of the paper manageable. It seemed to be an effective pricing strategy: Pricing based upon when the subscriber receives the news. The attractiveness of the pricing strategy was that anyone could afford *The Fleet Sheet*.

In order to ensure the timeliness of the paper, Erik initially guaranteed the larger companies that if they did not receive their fax of *The Fleet Sheet* before 9:00 a.m. each day, it would be free. However, the fax was never late, and Erik simply dropped this guarantee since no one worried about getting a fax late.

MARKETING OF *THE FLEET SHEET*

The marketing of *The Fleet Sheet* was multi-pronged. The first thing that Erik did was to advertise in English-language publications such as the *Prague Post*, *Business Central Europe* (published by *The Economist*), The American Chamber of Commerce Newsletter and in the Czech press in very select publications read by the elite. He was surprised that his subscribers had been not only people from English-speaking countries, but also the Dutch, French, German and even some Czech companies that realized having the news abbreviated for them saved valuable time.

The company also engaged in direct marketing. They found out about new companies moving to town from the American Chamber of Commerce, people Erik met, personal contacts and by word of mouth. With all new contacts, the company immediately apprised them of the product they were offering. Erik found that his satisfied subscribers let other people know about the service, and many new customers came from referrals. One reason his subscribers had been well satisfied was because Erik made an effort to dig into the important issues facing businesses in the Czech Republic. He also attempted to give people analysis rather than a simple reporting of the news. He found that clients read *The Fleet Sheet* because of the selection of articles that were covered.

The following testimonials by satisfied customers were published on the company's website:

The Fleet Sheet is far more than just a translation of Czech newspaper leads. With 20 years' experience behind him, the editor creates an unrivalled daily narrative of Czech life. It is the first thing I read every working morning. (Richard Hunt, Owner and Managing Director, Hunter Executive Search)

I don't always agree with what Erik Best writes, but I find it important to read everything he publishes, whether it is in *The Fleet Sheet*, the Final Word or the Friday Edition. (Andrej Babis, Chairman of the Board, AGROFERT HOLDING, a.s.)

The Fleet Sheet is short, quick and provides the key information I need to start my day. (Omar Koleilat, C.E.O., CRESTYL REAL ESTATE, s.r.o.)

A later addition to his marketing activities had been using email to whet the appetite of potential subscribers. (See Box 13.1 entitled "*The Fleet Sheet* Final Word.") Whenever anyone emailed him, Erik immediately added their name to a list of people who receive a summary of the day's *The Fleet Sheet* articles twice a week. The purpose of this was to acquaint them with the value of subscribing to *The Fleet Sheet* for daily faxes. Understanding the animosity some people have to receiving "junk emails," Erik added a notice at the bottom of the email that explained:

If you do not wish to receive such messages in the future, please simply let us know and we will remove your name from our list.

Few people ever asked to have their names removed, and many signed up as regular subscribers. This was probably because the email was only sent to individuals whom Erik believed would have an interest in Czech news.

In the late 1990s, Erik developed a website for his company. The web address was http:// www.fleet.cz. He believed that the website had enormous market potential for his company. It would now be possible for the company to place a page on the website that was a sampling of *The Fleet Sheet* for interested individuals and companies. Erik believed this had the potential to generate an even greater number of subscribers than did the email synopses.

In the past, Erik had offered the entire archives on disk. A company would pay about $500 a year to subscribe to the service. However, he decided to put all of his archives from the past on the website. The service was free, but one had to register to have access to it. This registry began to generate a good source of names for the email synopses which were intended to develop enough interest from the reader to cause him or her to subscribe to the fax service.

Erik hoped that his website would be of sufficiently high quality for people to continue to read it. He was gambling on the belief that a company could make more money in the long run by using its archives as a marketing tool to generate more subscriptions than by selling the archives as some companies such as the *Wall Street Journal* had done.

People occasionally asked Erik why he didn't go to email entirely as the medium for publishing and distributing *The Fleet Sheet*. His response was:

> There is the problem of protecting intellectual property. Unless you can encrypt it, you may have a copyright infringement of your material. In fact, one of Stephen King's stories which was published originally on the internet was encrypted, but someone broke the code. Another problem with encryption is that the message can only be sent to a specific person— not a company. Therefore, there were some real problems with encrypting the information on the internet.

HURDLES FOR THE BUSINESS

Unlike most startup businesses, *The Fleet Sheet* was profitable from the very beginning. Erik made an early decision to rent office space and computers initially. Whenever it became clear that *The Fleet Sheet* was a viable business, he did invest in some assets for the company such as necessary equipment.

Concerning the success of the company, Erik mused, "The revenues of the company have grown every year because the Czech Republic was seen early as the darling of the West, and they also received a great deal of media attention. Under more realistic conditions, many of the companies would not have come here." However, in the last couple of years there had been a decline in subscribers. Erik often contemplated how recent world economic events might be affecting the circulation of *The Fleet Sheet*.

As to the last hurdle, Erik commented:

> We have had to fend off 6 or 7 competitors who began to offer the same service that we were offering—a faxed bulletin with important political and economic news. It was a blatant rip-off of our product. The success of *The Fleet Sheet* drew other companies into the market.

Erik speculated:

> The drastic price reduction the competition offered in the beginning served to lower the overall revenue size of the market. I have often wondered if there is a big enough market to support ONE such publication over the long run, much less numerous competitors in a smaller revenue pool.

However, he also observed:

> The reason we survived was due to the overall quality of the paper. Business people know quality when they see it, and they immediately know that *The Fleet Sheet* is professionally done.

In the late 1990s, Erik decided to add an advertisement to *The Fleet Sheet*. The ad was priced at $400 a day and was rotated among four or five different companies' ads. If he should decide to add another advertisement, Erik would probably have to add another page to the fax. Faxing charges were minimal, the primary cost would be additional staff to prepare another page. However, he wondered if the primary focus of the paper—relevant information in a concise format—would be maintained. People don't mind taking the time to read one page of the most concise political and economic news of the day, but would they read two pages?

In the spring of 2007, there were around 1,000 subscribers to *The Fleet Sheet* paying an average of $2.50 each per day to receive the publication. In addition, each additional subscriber brought in 90 percent in profits and only 10 percent in variable costs. Erik speculated about whether a new format with two pages would reduce—rather than increase—subscribers.

Erik had always used Adobe Acrobat to format the paper, and the faxed paper was very easy to read. If he went to an email publication of the paper altogether, there could be a text format that would not be limited to one or two pages. But he wondered if that would affect the integrity of the product. They had done so well in the past with the concise format of a one-page fax. Would people sit at their computers and read through a lengthy email the way they read through a newspaper or fax that they can hold in their hands? Erik speculated, "If you could produce the same experience of reading a newspaper on the internet, it would be good. However, our present computer monitors prevent this from occurring." Erik also wondered how a company could build a brand name and attract a loyal readership over the internet. On the internet, one must click through so many pages to get to the desired material, that the opportunity cost of one's time becomes very expensive.

When Erik began his venture in 1992, he firmly believed it would be a short-term operation bridging the gap until a new economy was established and other sources of information became available. With that in mind, he had spent little time pondering an appropriate legal structure for the business. He had initially set the business up as a sole proprietorship, but now he wondered if he should have established it as an LLC. He would also have developed a long-term strategy for the company. He wondered if it was too late to develop a business plan for *The Fleet Sheet* and alter its legal structure. He knew he would have to fill out some forms and notify the United States government of his actions, but perhaps he should do that.

Erik wondered if a change in the legal structure of the organization would have capital gains tax implications if he decided to sell the business. He never assumed the business would last this long or he might have spent more time in planning rather than launching the business in two weeks.

ERIK'S DILEMMA

Erik wondered if this business could survive indefinitely into the future. He also wondered what factors would have an impact on the organization's remaining as a "going concern." Some foreign companies had already begun to close their offices in the Czech Republic because of the difficulties of doing business there, and the German banks were beginning to focus on Germany and not other countries. Even if the multinationals decided to stay in the country and there continued to be a market for *The Fleet Sheet*, he wondered what format it might take in the future. And then there was the question of the internet. Would people have such quick access to data on the internet that a service such as his would become obsolete?

Erik also thought about future competition. Would other companies try to offer the service he was offering at a lower price? Would subscribers be enticed by lower prices even though the quality of the product might be inferior?

When Erik had first begun his business, he was not making what he considered an adequate salary; and he often speculated that it would be very easy to close the business and go to work somewhere else. However, by the fall of 2019, the business was doing so well, and he was making a very good salary that it might be difficult to duplicate this operation somewhere else. Erik thought it strange to contemplate all of the problems that one encounters when a business becomes successful.

BOX 13.1 *THE FLEET SHEET* FINAL WORD

The Final Word is a short daily commentary on the major business and political issues affecting the Czech Republic. It's published Monday-to-Thursday each week by Erik Best and his experienced team and is free to anyone who chooses to subscribe. The Final Word has become an influential voice since it was founded in 2001. A Czech version of the Final Word has been available since 2010.

Each Friday, when the Final Word does not appear, we publish the Friday Edition, which is our weekly analysis of the main political and business events in the Czech Republic. It's included free with each subscription to *The Fleet Sheet* daily bulletin and is not available elsewhere (but you can sample a recent issue of the Friday Edition by clicking here.

The Fleet Sheet daily bulletin is our flagship product. It provides a quick and targeted look at the day's main news items and is read by most of the country's major companies. It's available by subscription only, but you may sample a recent issue by clicking here). You may also test it for a two-week period by registering for a Free Trial. Full access to *The Fleet Sheet* Archive is included with each subscription to *The Fleet Sheet* daily bulletin.

The Final Word Archive is free to everyone and includes all the individual articles published in the Final Word since 2001. It's an invaluable service and is available without registration.

The Fleet Sheet, Final Word and Friday Edition are serious products for anyone who is serious about succeeding in his or her field in the Czech Republic.

NOTE

1. Lyapura, Stanislav and Gibb, Allan A. (1996). Creating small businesses out of large enterprises. In J. Levitsky (ed.), *Small Business in Transition Economies*. London: Intermediate Technology Publications, pp. 34–50.

REFERENCE

Lyapura, Stanislav and Gibb, Allan A. (1996). Creating small businesses out of large enterprises. In J. Levitsky (ed.), *Small Business in Transition Economies*. London: Intermediate Technology Publications, pp. 34–50.

14

Preparing an exit strategy – BCH TeleCommunications: an American ex-patriot deciding when and how to leave the Czech Republic

http://www.bch.cz

Jeff Welker had come to the Czech Republic soon after the Velvet Revolution had wrenched control of the government away from the Communist Party and put it in the hands of Václav Havel (the famous dissident writer). He had tried out a number of innovative ideas, but all of them had failed to bring about the lasting entrepreneurial operation that he desired until he had launched BCH TeleCommunications in 1993. The company had at first delivered inexpensive callback services (discount calling services) to people living in the Czech Republic who wanted to call abroad. However, after callback services were no longer needed, Jeff had morphed his company into one that helped people with all types of telecommunications problems. Now it was January of 2020, and Jeff pondered whether he should remain in the Czech Republic with a successful company or return to the United States and find a job there.

BACKGROUND ON JEFF WELKER

For as long as he could remember, Jeff Welker had wanted to go into hospitality management. He completed high school in Glendale, California, and decided to enter the program at the University of Nevada at Las Vegas (UNLV). During his time at the university, he established many close relationships, including friendships with managers and directors of hotels in Las Vegas. With the conclusion of his work at UNLV, Jeff accepted a job as Assistant Convention Director at a Sheraton Hotel located in the Los Angeles area. With the next three years, Jeff was promoted several times. He reflected:

> Part of it was being in the right place at the right time, and part of it was giving 120 percent of myself. I had the people skills, the work ethic, morals, flexibility and ability to change when that was needed.

ENTREPRENEURIAL OPPORTUNITIES IN THE CZECH REPUBLIC

Jeff had made friends with a young lawyer from New York named Charles who was tired of the grueling hours in the large law firm in which he worked. In 1990, Charles planned to quit his job in order to start his own business; and Jeff was understandably startled when Charles asked him one day:

> Have you ever thought of building a hotel somewhere other than the United States for about 100 times less money? Do you know anything about the Riviera—the Yugoslavian Riviera?

Jeff admitted that he knew almost nothing about Yugoslavia, and he certainly did not know it had a Riviera. By a strange twist of fate, the travel section of the local newspaper had a two-page article on the Yugoslavian Riviera the following weekend. Jeff read each word carefully and began doing some research on this part of the world. He went to some investors he had in California who had said they would back him on any opportunity he could find to build or renovate a Premium Class hotel. His backers became just as excited as Jeff over this new opportunity. Unfortunately, war broke out in Yugoslavia in 1991 before they could get there, and this forced them to scrap the whole idea.

Four months later, Charles suggested that they should continue to concentrate on Eastern Europe where doors of opportunity were beginning to open for entrepreneurs. Charles proposed the idea of starting a bar and grill in Prague in what was then Czechoslovakia, which was viewed as the gateway between Eastern and Western Europe. Although he had never been there, Jeff had some knowledge of Czechoslovakia. Other circumstances in his life at the time caused him to rethink the future. He had moved from Sheraton Hotels to Marriott hotels, but now Marriott was in the process of restructuring. Jeff became uncomfortable with the changes he saw taking place. He decided Charles' idea was not so bad after all. He quit his job and began serious research on the new project.

RESEARCH FOR THE VENTURE IN PRAGUE

Although a formal business plan was never developed, Jeff and Charles did spend some time researching the proposed project in Czechoslovakia. Charles had decided that in addition to the bar and grill that Jeff would run, he would like to start an import–export business in Prague because he had always been enamored by this type of operation. He had a hunch that this business might work in a country newly opened to Western goods.

Charles needed to know about the types of goods not available in Czechoslovakia. First, at home in the library of the University of California at San Diego, they did some research on Czechoslovakia. Also, they visited the Czech Consulate in Los Angeles. Then they flew to Washington, DC and talked to the Czech Embassy, the United States Commerce Department, the EXIM (Export–Import) Bank, and the IMF (International Monetary Fund). They searched for information relating to the economic climate in Czechoslovakia. The Czech Consulate and Embassy told them there was a demand for used blue jeans and used computers. This was before widespread utilization of the internet. Research had to be personally conducted in libraries and people's offices. Charles' law firm had a one-person office in Prague, and that lawyer provided very useful and insightful knowledge about Czechoslovakia and other parts of Central and Eastern Europe.

Jeff and Charles began exploring names for their embryonic company and decided to use an acronym for the company name. After days of brainstorming, they selected the acronym BCH which was an abbreviation for "beach," a place where Jeff had spent some of the best years of his life. Later that year, Jeff and Charles arrived in Prague to launch their business operations. Jeff secretly wondered just where BCH Enterprises would take these two entrepreneurial friends.

THE VELVET REVOLUTION IN CZECHOSLOVAKIA

In November 1989, Czechoslovakia experienced what would later be referred to as the "Velvet Revolution." In response to the pleas of students and nurses, the socialist government finally stepped down and handed the country over to the people. Great social, political and economic changes subsequently occurred in the newly freed nation. The disintegration of the former Council for Mutual Economic Co-operation (Comecon) was one of the most significant factors for change. The National Assembly elected Václav Havel as President of Czechoslovakia on December 29, 1989.

The primary constraint to any reform efforts on the part of Václav Havel and his new government was the fact that all industrial and agricultural production was owned by the state or state-dependent collective farms. The new Minister of Finance, Václav Klaus, proposed in February of 1990 a coupon privatization project. By paying only a small administration fee, all Czechoslovakian citizens were given the opportunity to obtain a coupon book which could be used to purchase shares in certain privatized concerns. The first coupon books were sold on May 18, 1992 with the result that 70 percent of the population became shareholders. Following this, there was a project entitled "Small Privatization" which singled out smaller service and trade premises from state property and sold them at auction.

Another constraint to reform was the less than rapid integration of Czechoslovakia into the community of Western European states. Exporters in the Western European countries were delighted with the new opportunity to sell their goods in Czech markets, but they were disinclined to buy Czech goods. The former socialist economy was strongly oriented toward Comecon (a planned economy) and the Soviet Union. This had a negative effect on domestic production and caused the country to be non-competitive in world markets. The central planning commission stressed heavy industry and neglected the service sector entirely. Because of this, the Czech economy suffered a decrease in exports when Comecon was dissolved, and there was a loss of Eastern markets for their goods.[1]

Somehow the Czechoslovakian economy survived the break-up into the Czech Republic and Slovakia on January 1, 1993, and the collapse of markets in Eastern Europe. The country began to develop a greater orientation toward the markets of Western Europe, and more foreign firms began to enter the domestic Czech market.[2]

The government bureaucracy had become a major barrier to the creation of new enterprises. The former state-owned banks were very slowly being privatized and new banks from other countries were beginning to enter the country. However, the experience of one company in what was once Russia was very similar to experiences of entrepreneurs in the Czech Republic. This new small business received the required 27 documents, many requiring notarizations, after a loan approval and before the money could be disbursed.[3]

Two separate Czech economies appeared to be developing by the middle 1990s. One was the economy in which new Czech entrepreneurs were attempting to establish new ventures. They had great difficulty obtaining bank loans. They obtained bank loans if they were prepared to accept a 30 percent interest rate. Also, they had to break through the "old boy network" which was a residual of the socialist state. And the other sector which represented companies from Western countries that had access to banks outside the Czech Republic and well-skilled lawyers to assist with the bureaucracy, was experiencing great success. It was within this economic climate that Jeff and Charles hoped to start a business.

HURDLES FOR THE NEW BUSINESS

Many foreign companies that made investments in the Czech Republic became frustrated with the difficulty of getting things taken care of in a timely manner. Every contract or piece of paper needed a stamp by someone to make it official. Sometimes the stamps were paper stamps that could be purchased at a post office, and sometimes they were the imprint of a rubber stamp.

Jeff decided very early that he would not be daunted by such hurdles. He said to himself:

Look at yourself. You're no longer in America. You must do everything on your own and accept that.

Jeff believed that philosophy had saved him from many hours of anxiety fretting over the difficulty of moving processes along in his new country.

However, there were the hurdles that became insurmountable. With the import–export business, the hurdle was the incorrect information they had received from sources with whom they had consulted before entering the Czech Republic. Although they had been told by Czech sources that there was a great need for used computers in the Czech Republic; when they arrived, they found that most people who wanted a computer already had one. In addition, although there was a great demand for used blue jeans as had been suggested, any jeans that were imported were either stolen at the border or, if they made it past the border, were burdened with a heavy duty being placed upon them by the Czech government. Therefore, BCH could not make a profit with prohibitive duties on their products.

With the restaurant business, there were insurmountable hurdles with the renovation of the building to house the Bar and Grill establishment. Jeff and Charles signed a contract for a stated amount with one construction company only to have them come back later and suggest:

> We forgot to put doors and windows in our contract; and also there is water damage in the walls, and we have to fix that.

They let this company go and signed a contract with another construction company who later said to them:

> Oh, we must add an additional $80,000 to the contract for electrical wiring, elevators and stairs.

Jeff and Charles began to understand that the signing of contracts meant nothing, and the project would go well beyond their budget. They knew they could not continue to ask their investors to pour money into a black hole, so they gave up on the whole project. Jeff and Charles lost more than $40,000 on this project. Their deal with investors was that they would put $250,000 into the project, but they wanted Jeff and Charles to invest (and be willing to lose) the first $50,000. Jeff wondered if part of their problem might have sprung from the fact that neither of them spoke the Czech language and depended upon translators for all transactions.

AN INTRODUCTION TO CALLBACK SERVICES

Jeff began doing some hospitality management consulting in Eastern Europe. Tourism had become a big business after the demise of communism. He identified that a substantial expense was the cost of telephone calls. The Czech Republic had a metered charge for local and long-distance calls. At the time, the long-distance calling fee was $3.50 a minute (not sure where you got this number ... I believe it was much higher??). Jeff first used AT&T, then Sprint, then another carrier, but the costs were still quite high.

On a trip back to the United States, Jeff read in a magazine about a "Callback Service for International Calling." As soon as Jeff landed, he called a representative of the company, WorldLink Callback, and asked him to explain the meaning of "callback services." This representative commented:

> You call from Prague to our computer in New York to a specially assigned telephone number, and you hang up before our computer answers. After this, the computer calls you back and offers you a dial tone, and then you dial as if you were in the United States ... International rates in the United States are enormously cheaper than the rest of the world that they give you discounted rates.

When Jeff tried the process, it did not work exactly in the way stated by the representative. In 1992, only one out of ten phone calls worked in Czechoslovakia. Moreover, 99 percent of telephones in Czechoslovakia had rotary dials. When Jeff and Charles signed up for the service, they needed a touch-tone phone, but they had to bring one with them from the United States. Then they had to obtain an adaptor to make it work.

One day the Chief Executive Officer (CEO) of the company that offered callback services called them, and he asked if they would like the license for the service for Eastern Europe. Jeff immediately responded that they were not interested because he said:

Your service doesn't work; and if you want to know why, I will be glad to tell you.

The CEO responded:

Would you be interested if we got the service working?

Jeff said they might be interested. The CEO provided an engineer to listen to their complaints. When Jeff hung up the telephone, he said to Charles:

When people call you peddling a service, it turns you off. I have never liked selling, and I certainly didn't come to Prague to be a salesman.

As much as Jeff hated the idea of calling people and convincing them that they needed to buy their product, he and Charles reluctantly accepted the licensing and marketing agreement for the callback services in Eastern Europe. WorldLink Callback would be the first company to offer this service in Eastern Europe.[4]

Charles immediately began working on the project in May of 1993. Within four months, he had signed up 60 people. Charles went back to the United States for two weeks, and he asked Jeff to contact the firms he had sent information to concerning their services. Jeff made the follow-up calls. He telephoned people who had recently signed up for their service and asked, "How is the service doing?" At the time, the service provided by Czech Telecom (the former Czech monopoly) was poor. It took ten tries to get one call through. However, people using the service provided by Charles and Jeff reported a call got through seven out of ten times. His customers were very pleased with the service. All the companies that had received information from Charles indicated that they wanted to sign up for the service. All of this happened within 30 minutes, and Jeff was astounded.

After completing the calls, Jeff picked up the English language newspaper named *The Prague Post* which provided a synopsis of what was going on in Prague. He saw some advertisements placed by large multinational companies doing business in the Czech Republic. On a whim, Jeff randomly called some of the companies in order to explain the callback services provided by Charles and Jeff. The common response to his calls was: How fast can you send information and have a meeting with us?

Jeff hurriedly sent the information to the companies, met with them soon afterwards and very quickly signed them up for service.

THE COMPANY GROWS AND TAKES ON MORE STAFF

BCH TeleCommunications soon began to represent other telecommunications companies such as Sprint, Direct Net, Axcom, France Telecom and Dial International (DIT) who did not have a representative in Eastern Europe. The partners expanded the operations of BCH TeleCommunications into Poland, Slovakia and Hungary. In addition, Jeff expanded his hospitality management consulting into Slovakia and Hungary. A senior staff member of The Office of the Ministry of Finance identified BCH as one of the top new entrepreneurial companies in the Czech Republic. They sought Jeff's advice surrounding how to help Czech entrepreneurs succeed.

Jeff speculated that the success of BCH TeleCommunications was due to cheaper telephone services offered, and the good technical support provided to their customers. The company hired an engineer just to work on technical problems and help with future business expansion plans. Jeff noted that over 50 percent of their new business came from referrals by satisfied customers.

BCH TeleCommunications had excellent staff. Ivana, for example, started as a receptionist and within months she was a sales associate before becoming a director of the company. She was the person that Jeff relied upon to give a realistic assessment of the operations in the Czech Republic. Ivana was a Czech, and she knew better than Jeff what would work and what would not work in the Czech Republic. She was a native speaker and could assist with Jeff's learning of the Czech language. Also, Ivana was a trustworthy translator.

A CRISIS AND SHIFT IN MARKET OFFERINGS

Charles had become increasingly unhappy and frustrated with the business, and one day in 1995 he had left the country with all of the $150,000 that the business partners had in the bank and all of their legal papers. Jeff felt that the rug had been pulled out from under him. He normally had a very positive outlook on life, but this setback seriously upset him.

Jeff was able to keep the company going by contacting some of his customers who were late in paying and get their help by asking them to pay their bills so that he could continue to run the company. They did so, and his loyal employees stuck by him even though he had to delay paying their salaries.

Jeff began to realize that callback services were fading because of a saturation of the industry and a change in pricing by many of the mobile carriers around the world. The Federal Communications Commission in Washington was aware of the disparity in international dialing rates and enacted new pricing rules that forced foreign carriers to lower their rates or face possible punitive measures. Long-distance calling was getting cheaper, and Jeff saw the need for a change in strategy for his telecommunication business.

He decided to tap into the growing need for communication systems in hotels, apartment buildings and shopping malls. He shifted his emphasis to those target groups and began providing for their total needs in terms of communications and operations. Since he did not have all the resources he needed within his organization, he chose to outsource the technical part of this operation and hold on to the customer service portion and customer contracts of the business. This allowed him to keep the size of his staff small.

JEFF'S PERSONAL LIFE

Several years after arriving in Prague, Jeff had met a beautiful young Czech lady and had fallen in love with her. Soon thereafter, they had gotten married. In the next few years, their home was blessed with two little girls. Unfortunately, the marriage had difficulties and ended in a divorce. However, Jeff and his wife remained good friends and shared the parenting of their daughters. They were both heavily involved in the girls' activities including things that happened at school and after-school activities. One of Jeff's favorite activities was teaching the girls how to cook. He also loved the hours he spent playing games with them after school and on the weekends that he had them with him.

THE TELECOMMUNICATIONS INDUSTRY IN THE 2020s

The international telecommunications industry is in the mature stage of its life cycle.[5] In both developed and emerging markets, the industry was characterized by slow growth rates, market acceptance, industry consolidation and static service offerings. Over the 10 years leading to 2023, value added in the industry was expected to grow at an annualized rate of 4.4 percent which was slightly higher than global annualized GDP (gross domestic product) which was expected to grow approximately 3.4 percent during that period of time. The industry was also characterized by a very high rate of technology change and short technology life cycles.

The introduction of faster data transmissions had led to more bandwidth-intensive mobile applications (streaming music and video-on-demand), and these were the major drivers behind the rollout of 4G and 5G network technologies throughout the developed world. Consumer demand for wireless services was driven by macroeconomic factors including population and household income growth. A factor that could influence this demand was the predicted slowdown in world economies in the years immediately following 2019 because of the very long recovery period from the "Great Recession of 2008."

A DECISION TO MAKE

Jeff stood at the crossroads on January 1, 2020. He had told his friends that would be the day that he would begin to look closely at his life in Prague and make a decision about remaining there, returning to the United States where his family lived or even looking abroad to the Middle East to begin a business all over again. Prague had been good to him, and he had made many friends there. There was also the question about his girls. When each of them became 16, she could make the decision on whether to stay in Prague with her mother or go with their father wherever he might go, but that decision was still several years off for both of them. Jeff pulled out a yellow legal pad and wrote "Stay" at the top of one column and "Leave" at the top of the other column. Then he began working his way through the page.

NOTES

1. Radomin, J. (1999). An overview of the Czech Republic. *Czech Republic Business Guide*, Association of Foreign Investment, Prague 2, Czech Republic, pp. 2–6. The Czechs did not adjust or update their higher education curriculum to properly reflect and to teach Western business ideas/methods/skills. This was mirrored by most Czech companies, and; thus, many of the younger educated population had no understanding to the business ways of the West and how to interact in the Western business environment.

2. Pokorny, J. (1994). *The Czech Lands 1918–1997*. Prague, Czech Republic: Prague Press, pp. 41–46.

3. Wallace, E. (1996). Financial institutional development: The case of the Russian small business fund. In J. Levitsky (ed.), *Small Business in Transition Economies*. London: Intermediate Technology Publications, pp. 76–84.

4. A large contributing factor to signing the agreement was due to the poor results of any import/export business activities which Charles had believed he could build up.

5. IBISWorld (July 2018). World industry report. Global wireless telecommunications carriers. www.ibisworld .com/. Accessed October 24, 2018.

REFERENCES

IBISWorld (July 2018). World industry report. Global wireless telecommunications carriers. www .ibisworld.com/. Accessed October 24, 2018.

Pokorny, J. (1994). *The Czech Lands 1918–1997*. Prague, Czech Republic: Prague Press, pp. 41–46.

Radomin, J. (1999). An overview of the Czech Republic. *Czech Republic Business Guide*, Association of Foreign Investment, Prague 2, Czech Republic, pp. 2–6.

Wallace, E. (1996). Financial institutional development: The case of the Russian small business fund. In J. Levitsky (ed.), *Small Business in Transition Economies*. London: Intermediate Technology Publications, pp. 76–84.

INDEX

Abramovic, Marina 39
American Chamber of Commerce Newsletter 117
Aprovecho Research 102

B Corporation 57, 58, 60, 62
Baby boomers 70
Bain Capital 3, 6
Baio, Andy 38
bandwidth-intensive mobile applications 129
B&B Trash Services truck 19
BCH TeleCommunications
    callback services 126–7
    company grows and takes on more staff 128
    crisis and shift in market offerings 128–9
    entrepreneurial opportunities in the Czech
        republic 123
    hurdles for new business 125–6
    industry in 2020s 129
    research for venture in Prague 123–4
    Velvet Revolution in Czechoslovakia 124–5
Best, Erik 120
    education and early work experience 113–14
    The Fleet Sheet (*see The Fleet Sheet*)
biomass 101, 102, 111
Blackstorm Labs 30
Blumenthal, Neil 2, 3, 6, 9
brick-and-mortar stores 6–7
bridal dresses 76–7, 81
bridal stores in U.S. 79
Brown, Doug 67
Bush, George W. 16
business continuity plan 80
business incubators 12–13
"buy-one, give-one" model 2, 8

callback services 122, 126–8
carbon offset credits 105–7
CARES Act 69
Cash on Delivery Aid (COD Aid) 108
CCTs *see* Conditional Cash Transfers
CDM *see* Clean Development Mechanism
Chain Store 29
Chen, Perry 38
Clean Development Mechanism (CDM) 106
COD Aid *see* Cash on Delivery Aid
coffee shop 51, 67, 88
Cohen, Debra 6
commercial leasing industry 14–16
community-based approach 103

Conditional Cash Transfers (CCTs) 108
contact lens 7
copy-cats 5
cost-saving waste collection methods 23
Council for Mutual Economic Co-operation 124
crisis leadership competencies 71
crisis response stage 80
crowdfunding 41–3
customer service system 2
Cutler, Joel 5
Czech Republic 113, 114, 117, 118, 120, 122, 124,
    125–8
    entrepreneurial opportunities in 123
Czech Telecom 127
Czechoslovakia 114, 123, 126
    Velvet Revolution in 124–5

"Dapper Bear" 50
data management platform (DMP) 30
data protection 31
De La Soul 39
dedicated desk 12
Dees, J. Gregory 8
The Dharma Bums (Kerouac) 6
Dickerson, Chad 58, 62
"diffusion of innovation" model 41, 46, 47,
    109–11
Disney Fairy Tale Weddings Collection 76
DMP *see* data management platform
Dodd–Frank Act 16
"Don Giovanni" 114
"Doughnut Stores" 53
dynamic cookstove community adoption 109

Ebates 30
eBay 61, 62
e-commerce 6–7, 28–30, 57, 79, 93, 95
Economic Stimulus Act 16
effective pricing strategy 116
El Salvador 3
Ellis, Perry 75
emission-saving technologies 106
emotional roller-coaster 21
entrepreneur's time, pressure on 89
Environmental Protection Agency 23
Etsy 1, 57–8
    challenges for 62

competitors 61
direct competitors 61
income statements of 63–4
mission 59
outcomes 59
public offering 62
Three Bird Nest 59–61
EU Data Protection Directive 34
EyeFly 5
eyeglasses 2, 4, 6, 7
eyeglass frames 7
eyeglass industry 7

federal funding 7
Federal Reserve Board 16
Fenoli, Randy 78
financial resources, pressure on 89
Fixer Upper 51, 84, 85, 87, 88
The Fleet Sheet 113
     hurdles for business 118–20
     marketing of 116–18
     origination of idea for 114–15
     pricing strategy 116
     situation in Eastern Europe 115–16
Freddie Mac 15

Gaines, Chip 51, 84–5, 87, 88
Gaines, Joanna 51, 84–8
GDPR *see* General Data Protection Regulation
General Data Protection Regulation (GDPR) 31, 34
Generation Z 70
Gilboa, David 2, 3, 5, 8
GMS *see* gross merchandise sales
GoFundMe organization 42
Gordon Brothers Capital 75
Grayson, Nancy 67
"Great Recession" 11, 14, 15, 33
greenhouse gas emissions 106
Grepper, Ryan 40
groom's attire 82
gross merchandise sales (GMS) 57, 59

Havel, Vaclav 124
Hisrich, Robert 88
home improvement contract referral service 6
hot desk 12
human resources, pressure on 89
Hunt, Andrew 2
Hyakuno, Kentaro 29

Ibisworld.com 95
Iman 8
indie game developer's plea 45
Indiegogo 42, 43
inefficient biomass-burning methods of cooking 102
initial public offering (IPO) 12, 29, 57, 61
international telecommunications industry 129
IPO *see* initial public offering

James, Erika Hayes 70
Japan 28–30, 34
     declining economy 32–3
     declining population 33
Jedda, Frank 77
Jimmy Fairly 5

Kalin, Robert 57, 58
Karan, Donna 75
Kerouac, Jack 3
     The Dharma Bums 6
Kickstarter 38
     community 39
     crowdfunding 41–3
     diffusion of innovation model 46, 47
     evaluation of 43
     funded projects 40–41
     funding sources for each venture stage 44
     game designer's plea to potential funders 44–5
     indie game developer's plea 45
     mission 39
     plea from inventor of scentplay 45–6
     problems 41
King, Stephen 118
Kleinfeld Bridal
     appointments 76
     background of owners 75
     bridal dresses 76–7, 81
     bridal stores in U.S. 79
     coronavirus pandemic 80
     crisis management 80
     groom's attire 82
     history of 74–5
     interesting facts about 76
     Men's store 77
     pop-up shop in New Jersey 77
     Say Yes to the Dress 77–8
     wayfair revamped dressing rooms 77
Kors, Michael 75
Kowalke, Jordan 101, 102, 106–9

Krux DMP 30
Kyoto Protocol 106, 107

lab desk 12
"landfill-gas-to energy" 24
LensCrafters 7
Lily Jade 1, 92
    diaper bag 96
    employees 95
    filling orders 94
    imposter 93
    industry outlook 95
    launching 93
    operating in China 94
    social media analytics 97–9
    The Sourcing King 93
    using social media 94–5
Lunch & Learn sessions 12
Luxottica 7
    business model of 3

Made Eyewear 5
Magnolia 1
    businesses 85–7
    challenges for firms 88–9
    farms 89
    market 85
    network 88, 89–90
    tree 84
Maguire, Chris 57
management of employees, pressure on 89
management training program 18
market offerings, crisis and shift in 128–9
McKelvey, Miguel 11
Medicaid 7
Medicare 7
"meet and greet" events 95
membership 12
Mikitani, Hiroshi 28, 30, 32
Mizrahi, Isaac 75
Mulpurn, Sucharita 6

National Basketball Association 30
Nelson, B.J. 18–20
Nelson, Scott 18–20, 24, 25
Neumann, Adam 11
New Century Financial 15
Nightlight Donuts 1
    COVID-19 pandemic 54
    decision time 54
    industry background 53
    new business 50–53

    possible location for 56
    profit and loss statements 55
    Wren twins 49–50

Oakley stores 7
OBA see out-put based aid
Obama, Barack 15, 16, 38
"office hoteling" 14
Office Hours 12
office leasing industry in U.S. 14–15
office spaces 12–13
online travel markets 30
out-put based aid (OBA) 108
outsourcing 5–6

Paris Agreement of 2015 106, 107
Parker, Zagg 3
Patel, Amit 29
Payroll Protection Program (PPP) 69, 80
Pearle Vision 7
Pebble smartwatch 40
People Search 58
Pepper, Warby 3
PforR see Program-for-Results
post-acquisition support 109
post-crisis stage 80
PPP see Payroll Protection Program
Prague, research for venture in 123–4
pre-crisis stage 80
private health insurance 7
private investment groups 105
private office 12, 16
Program-for-Results (PforR) 108
project model for carbon 110
Pupil Project 8

R Games 30
Raider, Jeffrey 2
Rakuten 35–6
    additional acquisitions and launches 29–30
    alliance with Walmart 30
    collecting customer data 31
    General Data Protection Regulation (GDPR) 34
    Japan's declining economy 32–3
    Japan's declining population 33
    offerings to merchants 28–9
    problems for company 32
    public offerings 29
    shopping secrets survey 32

sports investments 30–31
Rakuten Kobo 29, 30
Rakuten Pay 30
Ray-Ban 7
RBF *see* results-based financing
regulatory markets 106
"re-imagining of commerce" 58
Remedies 16
residential trash service 21
results-based financing (RBF) 106–8
Reverb 59
Revival Restaurant 1, 66
    business plan 67
    coronavirus pandemic 69–70
    crisis management 70–71
    decision 71
    employees 68
    exterior of 71
    food sourcing 69
    gentrification 68
    location 67–8
    menu 72
    single location restaurants in U.S. 70
Rodriguez, Cherri 62
Rogers, E.M. 46, 110
Rothstein, Ronnie 75, 78

Say Yes to the Dress 75, 77–8
SBA *see* Small Business Administration
Schacter, Jack 74
Schoppik, Haim 57
"shadow space" 14
Silos 1, 84–6, 88
Silverman, Josh 62
Simms, Stuart 30
small and medium-sized business enterprises
    (SMEs) 29
Small Business Administration (SBA) 69
small business textbooks 1
"Small Privatization" 124
SMEs *see* small and medium-sized business
    enterprises
Smith, Adam 114
"social distancing" 69, 74, 79
social entrepreneur 2
social entrepreneurship model 8
social media 94–5
    analytics 97–9
social responsibility programs 105
soft economy 14
"The Sourcing King" 93
sovereign donors 104–6
sports investments 30–31
Steinem, Gloria 8
stimulus package 16
sunglasses 4, 5, 7

Sunglass Hut 7

Taiwan Rakuten Ichiba 29
tenants 12
The Learning Channel (TLC) 77, 78, 108
"thermal efficiency" 104
Three Bird Nest 59–61
TLC *see* The Learning Channel; Total Land Care
TLC Rocket Stove 105
    carbon offset credits 106–7
    challenges to adoption 108–9
    cooking in Africa 101–2
    "diffusion of innovation" 110–111
    interventions 103
    Jordan Kowalke 102
    mission 103
    organization and employees 103–4
    problem 109
    program design and implementation 103
    project model for carbon 110
    results-based financing (RBF) 107–8
Tohoku Rakuten Golden Eagles 30
Tom's Shoes 8
Total Land Care (TLC) 101, 102–4
traditional bridal store 79
troubled asset relief program 16
Trump, Donald 11
Trust and Safety Team 42

United Nations Framework Convention on
    Climate Change 106
United States Agency for International
    Development (USAID) 103, 105
Urshel, Mara 75, 77

value proposition 4
Velvet Revolution in Czechoslovakia 122, 124–5
Venture Initiation Program 3
VisionSpring 3, 8
voluntary carbon credits 106
voluntary markets 106, 107

Waco Tribune-Herald 11
Warby Parker 1, 2–3
    copy-cats 5
    e-commerce *vs.* brick-and-mortar stores 6–7
    employees 6
    eyeglass industry 7
    Luxottica 7
    mission 4
    outsourcing 5–6
    product 4–5
    social entrepreneurship model 8
    value proposition 4
waste collection services 22, 23

Waste Management company 18–19, 24, 20
waste services industry 22–3
Wayfair Registry 77
Welker, Jeff 122–9
    BCH TeleCommunications (*see* BCH
        TeleCommunications)
"wet market" 80
WeWork 11
    great recession 15–16
    office leasing industry in U.S. 14–15
    office spaces 12–13
    shared office space pricing 13
    workplace office space trends 13–14
White Trash Services 18, 19
    assets in 2020 21
    considerations in municipality bidding 24–5
    decision 25–6
    dumpster 26
    finances 20–21
    operations 20

    percentage of business 21–2
    residential containers 25
    roll-off dumpster 26
    waste management company 24
    waste services industry 22–3
WHO *see* World Health Organization
wireless services, consumer demand for 129
Wood, Meggan 92–6
workspace allocation 13–14
World Health Organization (WHO) 69, 80
WorldLink Callback 126, 127
Wren, Eric 49–51
Wren, Jackson 49–54
Wunder, Seth 62

Young, Danielle 66–9, 71
Young Life 66, 73

Zelnik, Michel 74
Zito, Tony 30